LOST GILLINGHAM

PHILIP MACDOUGALL

AMBERLEY

To my granddaughter Millie, born in Gillingham, February 2023

First published 2024

Amberley Publishing
The Hill, Stroud
Gloucestershire, GL5 4EP

www.amberley-books.com

British Library Cataloguing in Publication Data.

A catalogue record for this book is available from the British Library.

ISBN 978 1 3981 1748 8 (print)
ISBN 978 1 3981 1749 5 (ebook)

Typesetting by Simon and Sons, India.
Printed in the UK.

Contents

Introduction

Lost Gillingham looks at the Gillingham that is no more, the way things were and the buildings and traditions that have simply slipped away. In the Middle Ages and earlier, those who lived in the parish were mainly clustered around a small village close to St Mary's – 'the Church on the Green'. Most other land within the parish was farm or waste land. Admittedly there were a few additional settlements. Among them to the east was the Manor of Grange, where a monastic house had once been established, while to the west, close to where the dockyard was to be later built, was Westcourt Manor. To the north, along the banks of the river, fishing provided a living for some families, and to the south, alongside the old Roman road (Watling Street, now the A2), a small number gained an income from meeting the needs of hungry travellers or those desirous of a bed for the night.

Only later, during the reign of Henry VIII, did Gillingham begin to see any real change. Suddenly, and for those living in the village somewhat unexpectedly, the Navy arrived. They decided that the River Medway was a good and safe place for the harbouring of the king's ships. Not many, admittedly, but it was to 'Jyllingham water' that King Henry ordered them. On shore and supporting those ships, storehouses are mentioned, their use giving new opportunities to those living close to the shoreline, mainly families that were dependent on fishing. Some would have embraced the opportunity of working as storehouse labourers, while others would have used fishing boats to ferry men and materials to and from the ships moored within sight of the village. Among them was almost certainly the parents of Will Adams, the Gillingham mariner, born in 1564, who later sailed to Japan. In describing the village in which he was born, Adams was to write of it as lying 'two English miles from Rochester and one mile from Chatham, where the King's ships do lie'.

Just as suddenly as the Navy arrived in Gillingham, so it departed. From 'Jyllingham water', during the reign of Elizabeth I, the Navy transferred itself away, moving further upriver towards Chatham. Here in 1571, under the shadow of the church of that parish, also named St Mary's, a dockyard was opened. But for Gillingham, all was not lost. The distance to the new yard was not so great, being that it was walkable. In recruiting a workforce for the building and repairing of ships, men from Gillingham would have willingly sought employment in the yard – some as shipwrights, and others with lesser skills were also made welcome.

A further turn of events came in the 1620s. In that decade, on the site of the present-day Historic Yard, a new and much larger dockyard was built, entirely replacing the one built fifty years earlier. This new yard, quite literally, was within a stone's throw of the boundary with Gillingham, and for those employed in that yard, Gillingham became the favoured place for a family home. To be more precise, it was not just anywhere in Gillingham that was so favoured, but the land belonging to the Manor of Westcourt, upon which the community of Brompton would later emerge. Over time, the various owners of Westcourt, including Thomas Rogers, who acquired the manor in 1698, began selling off plots of land for houses, to be occupied by those mainly employed in the yard.

It was that same dockyard, while initially lying outside the parish of Gillingham, that was to be the controlling factor on the growth and development of Gillingham's various isolated settlements and the eventual combining of these settlements into one heavily concentrated township. However, for Brompton, one problem certainly hindered a smooth outward development: the community here was effectively trapped, hemmed in on one side by the dockyard and on the other by a defensive ring known as the Lines. The latter was an extensive area, mostly open ground, set aside for the purpose of providing an open field of fire for the army should it be called upon to defend the yard from an attacking enemy. For this reason, the continued demand for housing by those employed in the dockyard was impossible for Brompton to satisfy; any land adjoining this community was simply not available for house construction. Instead, demand had to be met by a process of leapfrogging across the Lines to approximately a mile to the east, where there was undeveloped land belonging to Britton Farm. Here, although not until much later, the High Street would be built, while Britton Street, the now closed Britton Farm House pub and Britton Farm Mall would all later serve as reminders of the one-time existence of that earlier farm that once lay within the parish of Gillingham.

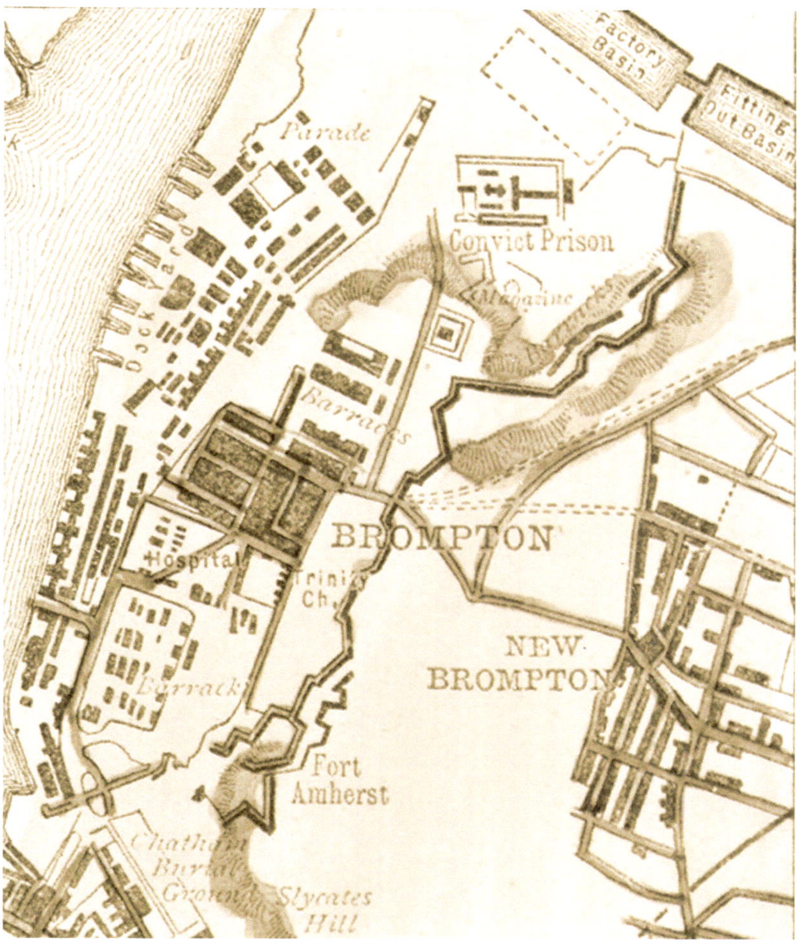

A late nineteenth-century map showing the two communities of Brompton and New Brompton, as central Gillingham was then known, together with the location of the Lines and the naval dockyard.

Of course, the owners of Britton Farm at first saw only a limited demand for plots of land, the entrance to the yard up until the mid-nineteenth century being on Dock Road in Chatham, and so some distance from land belonging to the farm. Later came yet one more sudden dramatic turn of events: the Navy, courtesy of a major Victorian-age extension, which was to triple the size of the existing dockyard, was brought back to Gillingham, with most activities in the yard now centred on Gillingham – or rather the Gillingham extension. To access this massive addition to what would still be known as Chatham dockyard, new entrance gates were established in Gillingham, creating an almost limitless demand for land within the parish, on which more houses and other amenities would be built. The owners of Britton Farm, as noted, were among those who took up the challenge, selling out big-time to property developers. Seen more as an extension of Brompton rather than that of the original village of Gillingham (as it was based around St Mary's on the Green), the developments taking place on land formerly belonging to Britton Farm, as well as the immediate surrounding area, became known as New Brompton.

Soon, hundreds of new properties were under construction, and lines of streets began to emerge. Often the houses were built by their owners and future occupiers with few rules governing the process. At this time New Brompton lacked any firm municipal authority, so planning rules were not just lax but simply non-existent. Buildings therefore took on a myriad of styles and a similar variation in quality. It was not until the Local Government Act 1894 that a legalised municipal borough was created, an authority which abandoned the name New Brompton, adopting instead the name of Gillingham. It was this newly created borough, through powers bestowed on it by Parliament, that finally brought about order to a town that had grown so rapidly that in appearance, it at one time seemed more akin to the 'Wild West' than a nineteen-century English community subservient to careful forms of organisation.

As the numbers employed in the yard continued to grow, the number of houses continued to multiply, with those dating to around the 1870s built closest to the new Gillingham Gate, but by the turn of the century had spiralled outwards, with those more distant from the dockyard, such as Balmoral Estate (Windsor Road, Balmoral Road and Buckingham Road), constructed at the turn of the century. By now Gillingham had become, in terms of population, the largest town in Kent. Still the outward sprawl of housing continued, helped by the advent of trams, followed in turn by petrol-driven buses, leading to mass housing schemes along Duncan Road/Nelson Road and, during the interwar years, further outward towards the A2.

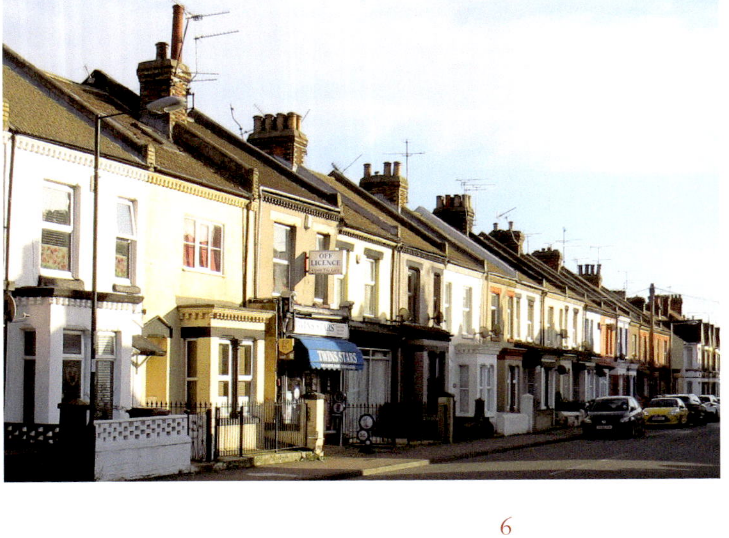

Housing built at the turn of the century: the Balmoral Estate.

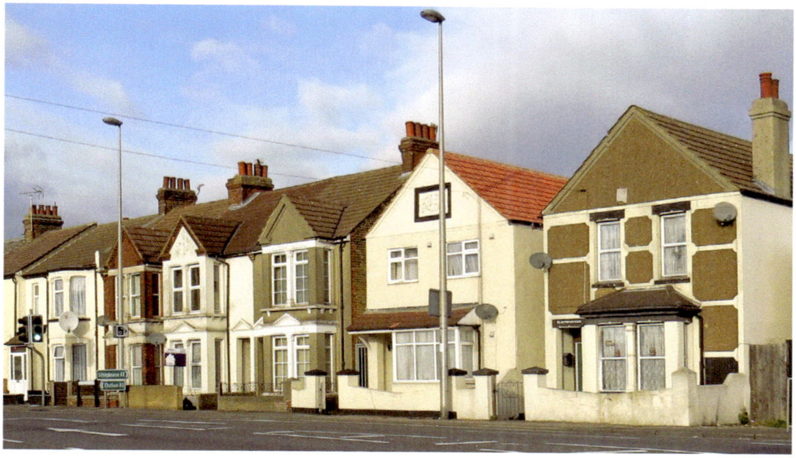

Housing built during the interwar years to accommodate the workforce of a still expanding dockyard: Watling Street.

This then is Gillingham of the past, a parish once shaped by the Navy and the dockyard that supported it. A town that, up until final closure of the dockyard and adjoining Royal Naval Barracks, had been totally subsumed to the needs of the Navy. All this changed in 1984; the closure of the dockyard and barracks ripped the heart out of the town and all for which it had once proudly stood. Many families had to move, forced to find employment elsewhere. In all, more than 7,000 workers lost their jobs, along with another 10,000 in associated industries. Slowly, however, along with the rest of the Medway, Gillingham has slowly recovered from what was effectively a knockout blow. Substantial financial investment eventually arrived, much of which was used to bring about a complete redevelopment of St Mary's Island, the land on which much of the nineteenth-century dockyard extension had been built. Here there is now over a thousand new homes, with yet more in the pipeline. In addition, finally approved in 2013, there is a £650 million redevelopment scheme for part of the former dockyard, the area that came into the hands of Medway Ports Authority (Port of London Medway), with the project, despite lying fully within Gillingham, adopting the name Chatham Waters. It is a project that includes office space, education facilities, flats, townhouses and a superstore.

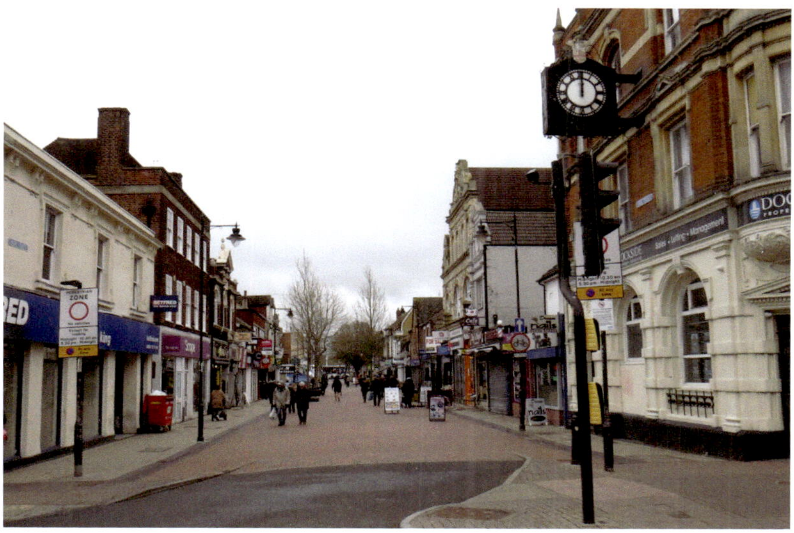

Today, the community of Gillingham continues to thrive despite the loss of the dockyard some forty years ago, which was then the heart of the community.

I

Early Years

Before the arrival of the Navy, the parish of Gillingham was little different from most other country parishes, other than its proximity to the River Medway. This made it possible for some families to survive on fishing and the trawling of the river for seafood. In pre-industrial days the Medway was a free-flowing river teeming with fish – smelt, perch, pike and carp were very common in those days. Things changed after the arrival of the Navy. While fishing was still profitable, the Navy now provided those who lived in Gillingham with alternative employment, as well as the thrill of seeing the king's ships regularly moored in the nearby river.

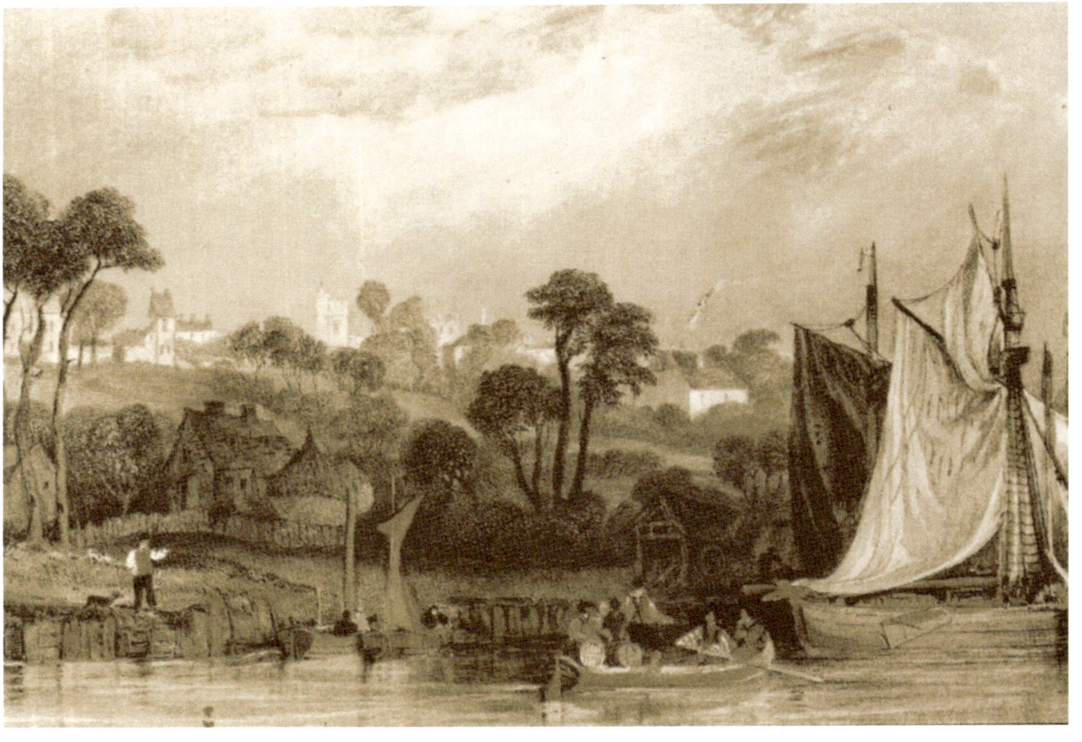

The riverside area of Gillingham looking towards the village as it once appeared – a picture of peace and tranquillity.

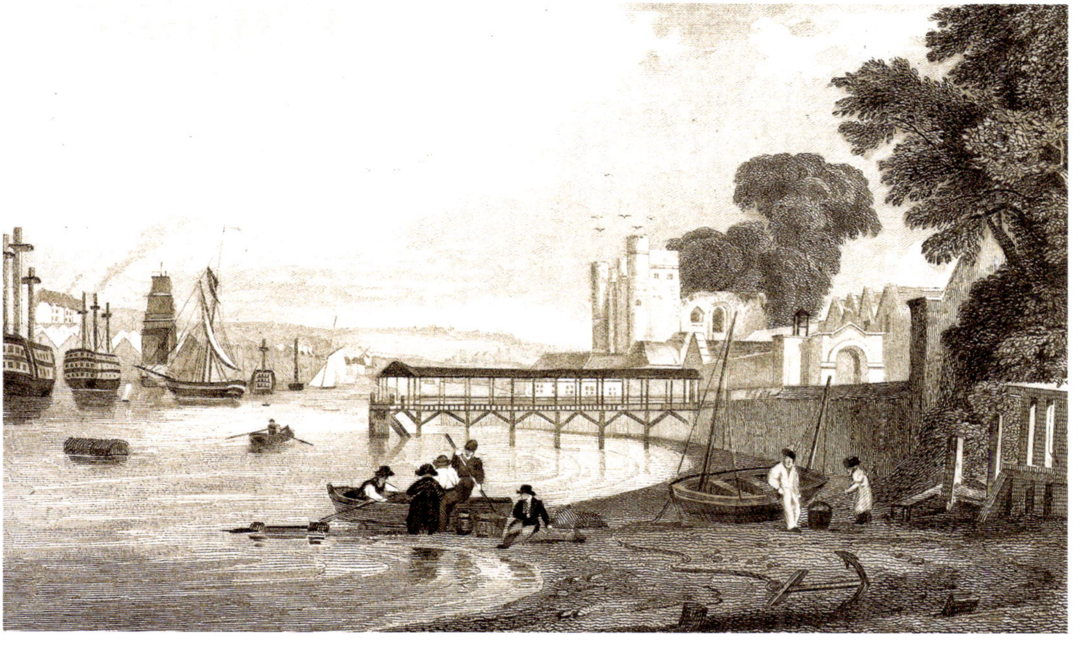

Seen here during the early nineteenth century, the Medway as it runs past Gillingham. Despite the Navy having taken occupancy of the area several centuries earlier, it is still a scene that reflects peace and calmness – almost idyllic. A few warships are seen moored within a stone's throw of the Gillingham shoreline, while Upnor Castle holds majestic sway on the opposite bank of the river.

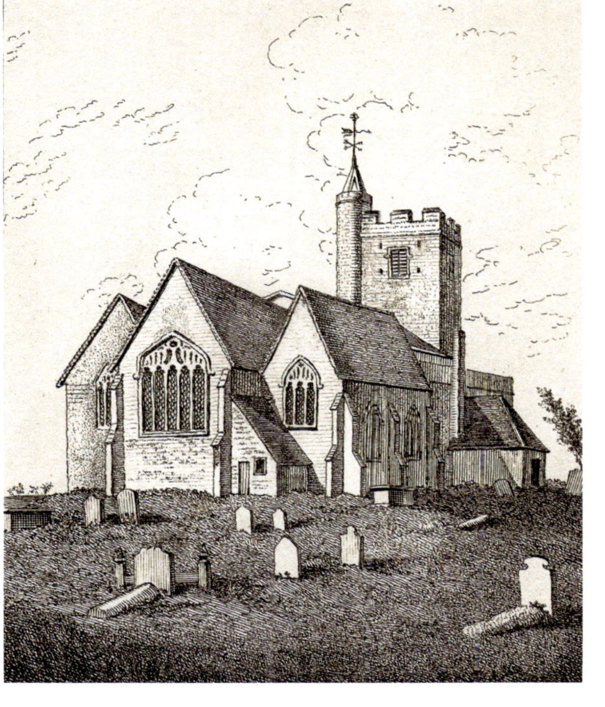

The parish church of St Mary Magdalene – 'the Church on the Green' – seen here during the nineteenth century. The church, once the centre of the parish, became somewhat isolated in later years, the dockyard creating, in its need for a constantly expanding workforce, two new communities on the far west side of the parish – Brompton and New Brompton.

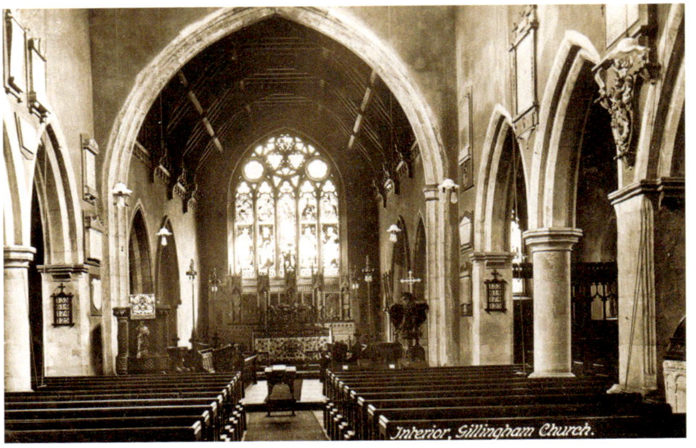

An early twentieth-century interior view of St Mary's Church. While much of what can be seen dates to the fifteenth century, the church also contains stonework dating back to the early fourteenth century or possibly earlier.

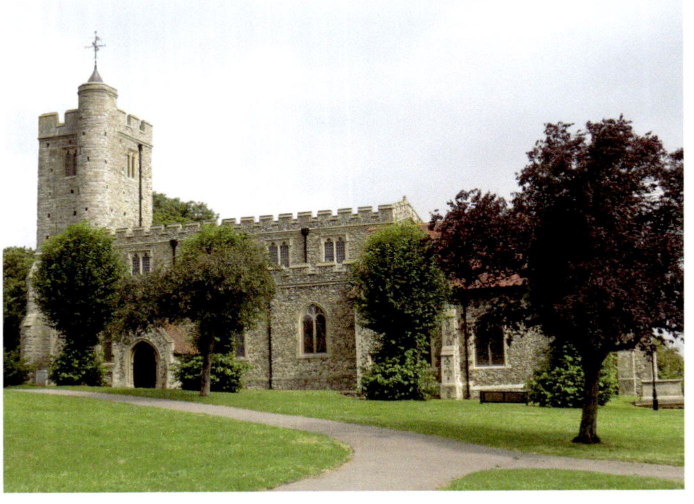

A modern-day view of St Mary's Church as seen from the south-east. Gillingham as a settlement goes back to at least Saxon times, and is mentioned in the Domesday Book of 1086 when it possessed a total of sixty-nine households or families. This suggests a total population of somewhere between 250 and 350.

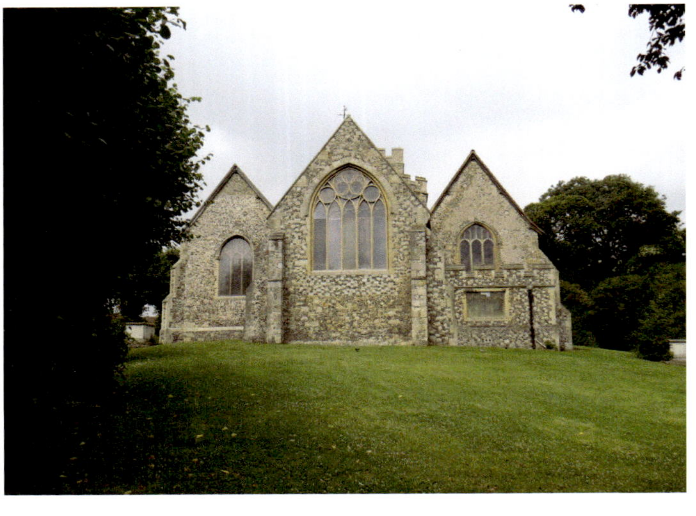

The eastern end of St Mary's Church. Will Adams, one of Gillingham's most famous characters, the first Englishman to set foot in Japan, was baptised in this church on 24 September 1564.

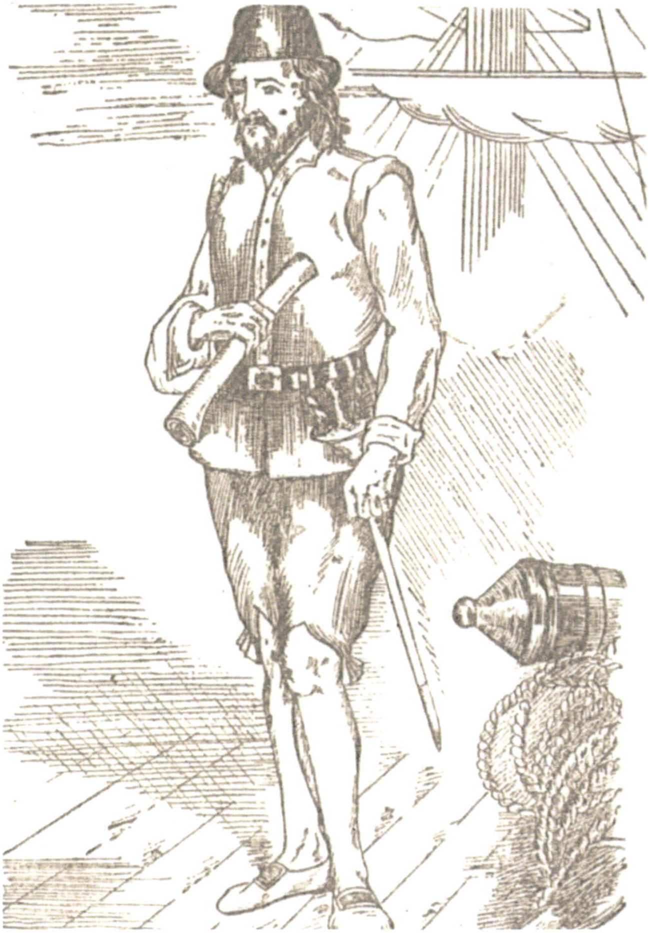

Will Adams as he is presumed to have appeared in 1598, the year in which he set out on a trading expedition that would bring him to the coast of Japan, where he was shipwrecked. As the holder of a Trinity House license he had been appointed pilot-major of a Dutch expedition, the object of which was to establish trading links with various Far East nations.

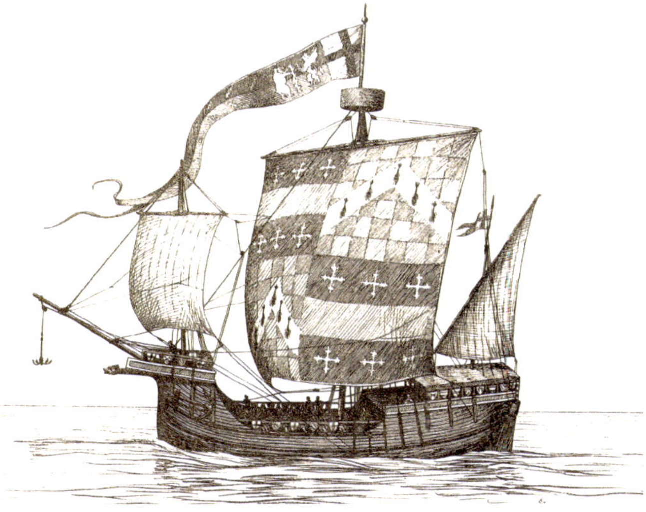

It was during the reign of Henry VIII that the Navy first arrived in 'Jillyngham water'. Vessels similar to the one seen here began mooring just off the village and parish of Gillingham. Storehouses for naval use were hired in 1547 at a cost of thirteen shillings and four pence per year.

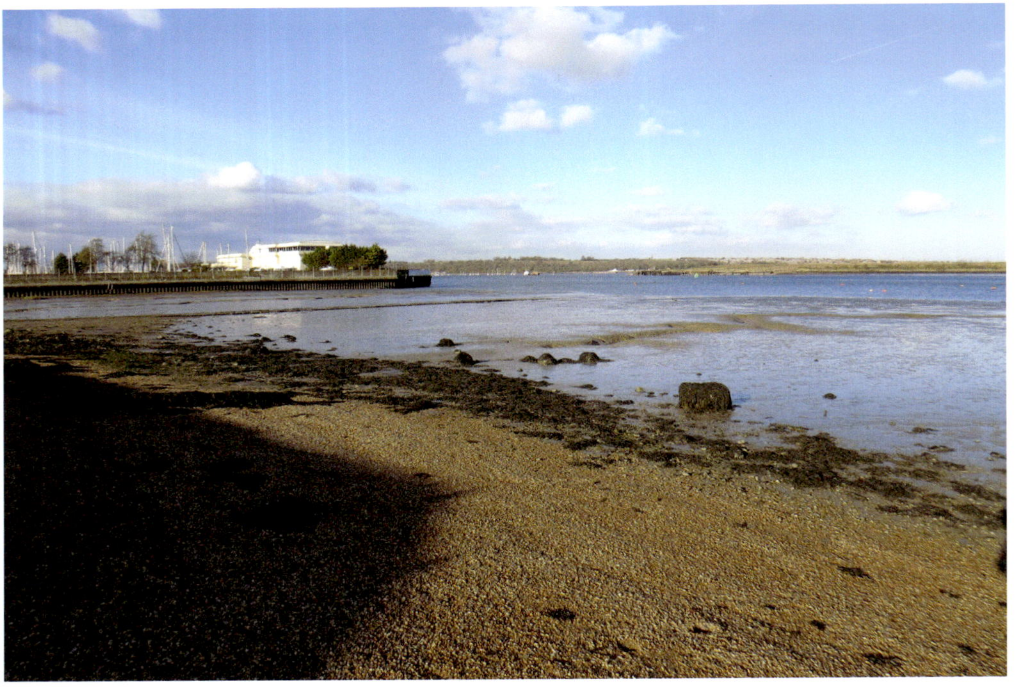

The River Medway off Gillingham where Henry VIII once moored the ships of his navy. Here they were well protected from enemy attack, but relatively close to London, where ordnance and other supplies could be readily obtained.

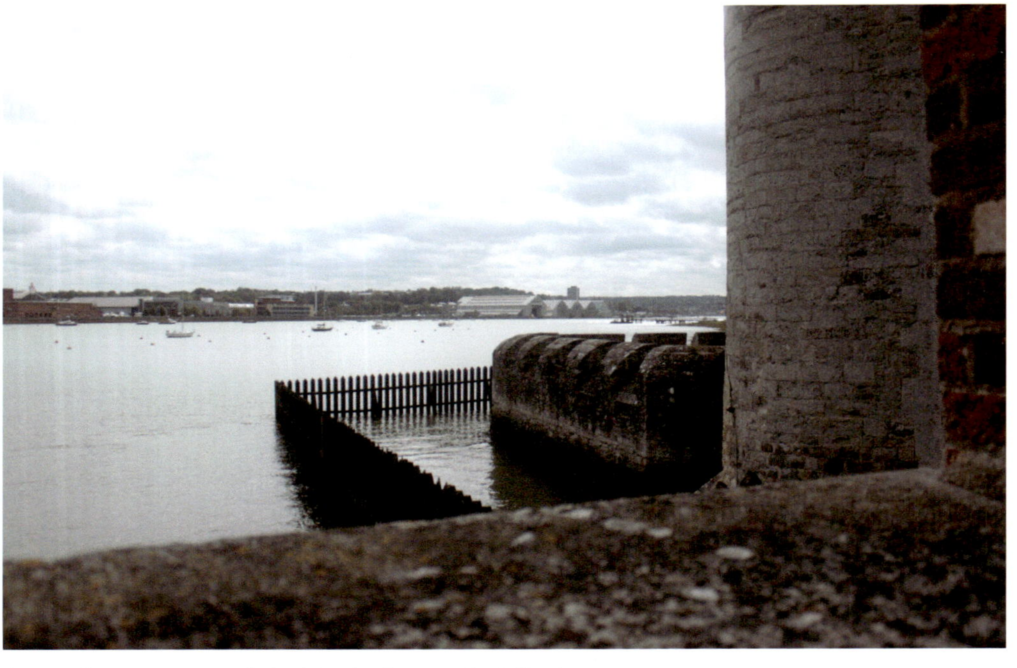

A view from Upnor Castle looking back towards Gillingham.

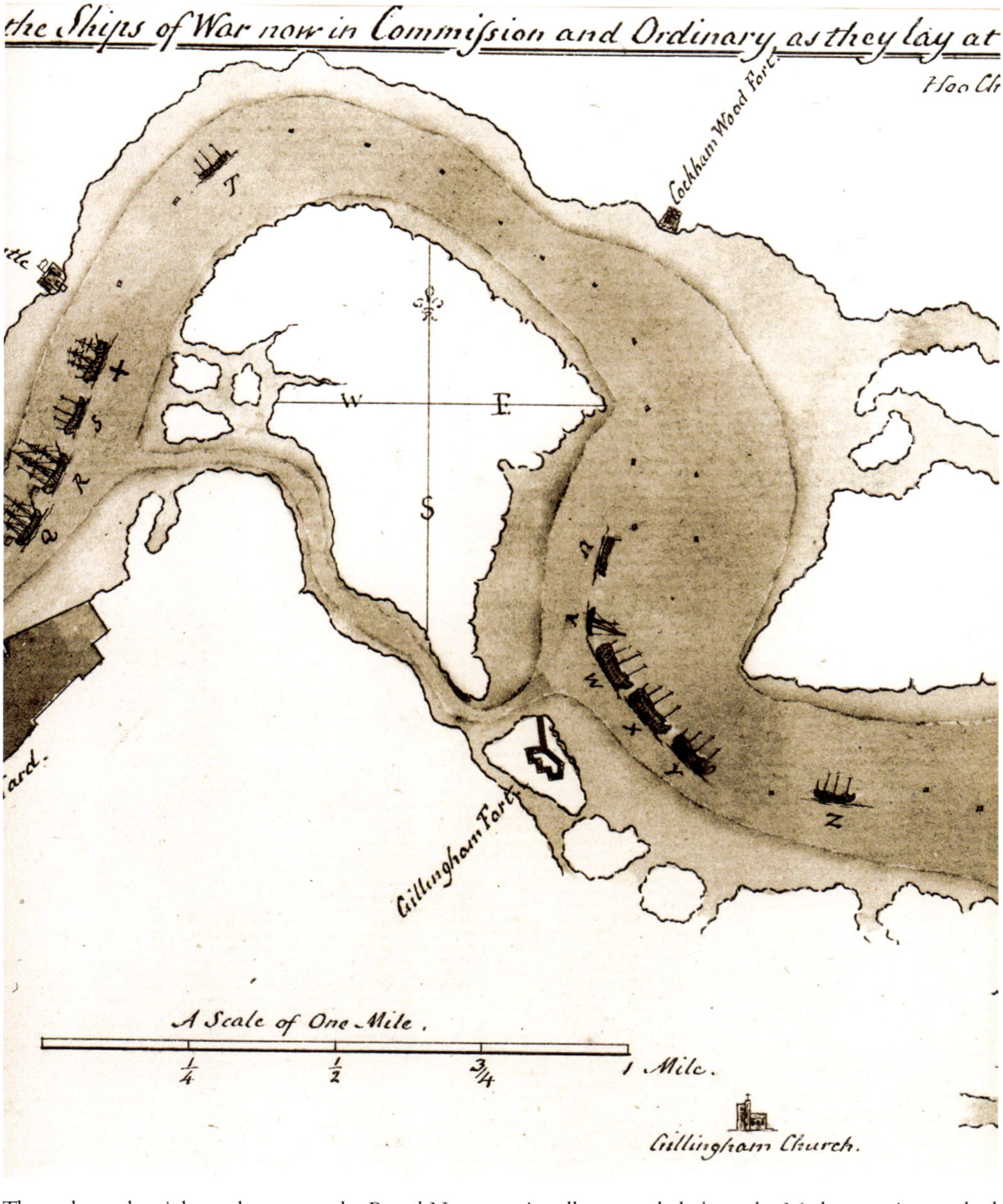

Throughout the eighteenth century, the Royal Navy continually expanded along the Medway as it stretched past Gillingham, and as shown by this chart dating to the mid-eighteenth century, it was utilised as a mooring point for a great many capital ships. They would stay here during times of peace, maintained by the workforce of the dockyard, who would also quickly ready them for sea upon the outset of war. For residents of Gillingham in those years, these ships must have presented a truly fascinating sight, but in doing so they also heralded a worrying prospect. For when war broke out, these ships had to be manned, with the Navy quick to scour the shoreline to force any man found between the ages of eighteen and fifty-five years (and who had 'used the sea') to serve on those ships. Many an unwary Medwayer must have been caught by what were known as press gangs. Only those who could prove themselves a gentleman or had exemption papers could, if apprehended by a press gang, avoid many years of sea service under the most gruelling of conditions.

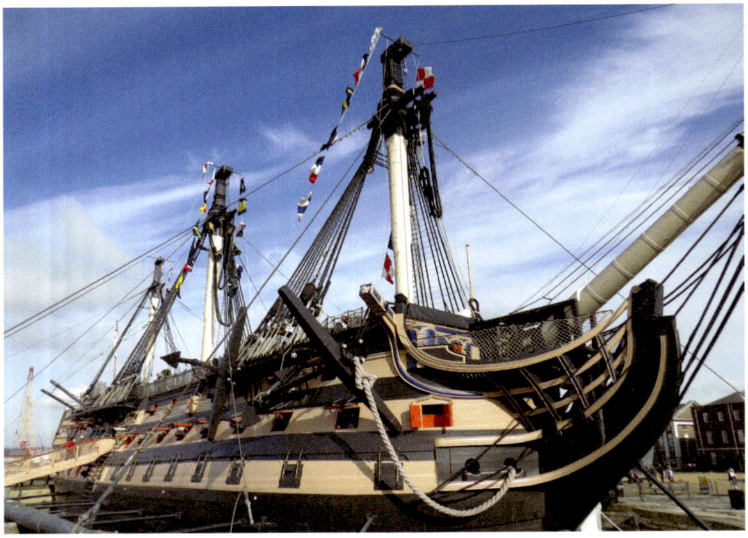

Among the major warships moored close to Gillingham during the late eighteenth century was Nelson's future flagship at Trafalgar, HMS *Victory*, seen here at Portsmouth, her final home. Built in the dockyard at Chatham, it was launched in 1765. With no immediate demand for the ship to enter naval service, she was to remain moored off Gillingham until placed on active service in 1778 during the American War of Independence.

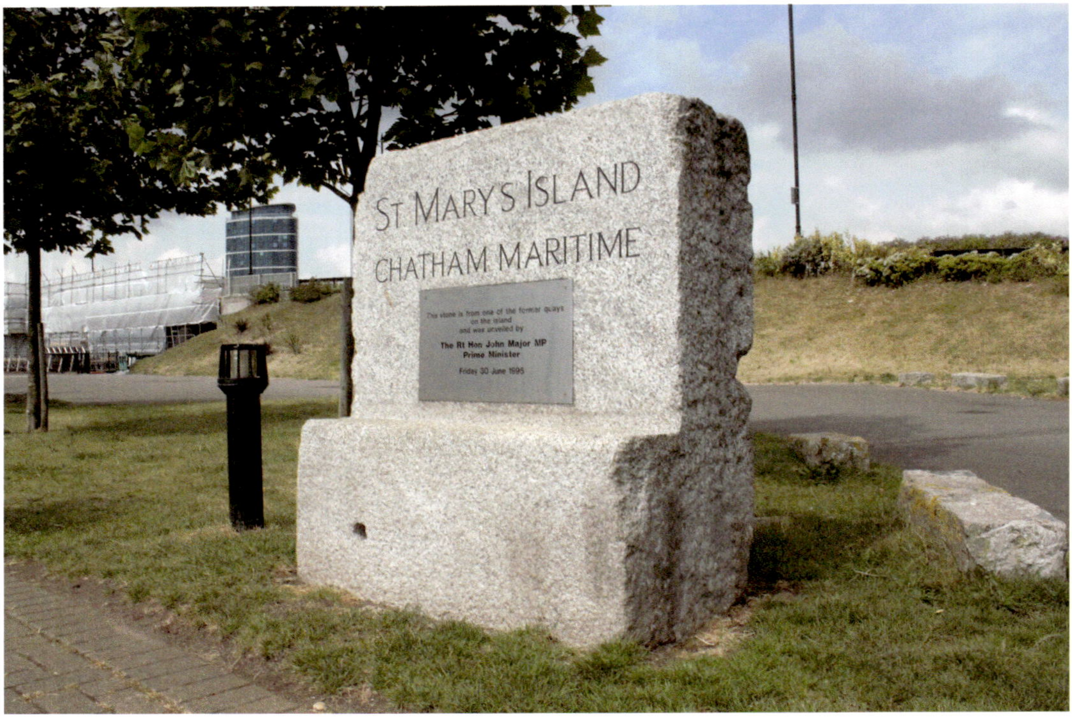

St Mary's Island was once nothing more than an extensive area of freshwater marshland known as Finborough Marsh. Unhealthy to the few that lived on the island, there being few tenements at that time, it was to be completely transformed during the third quarter of the nineteenth century by providing land for the massive extension to the dockyard at Chatham. Initially, part of St Mary's Island was purchased by the Admiralty in 1810; at that time, it was used for dumping mud dredged from the river when securing safe navigable channels for the larger warships coming into the river.

Today St Mary's Island, following redevelopment of the former dockyard, has been totally transformed. Along its shoreline it offers occasional memories of the former dockyard together with excellent views of the river.

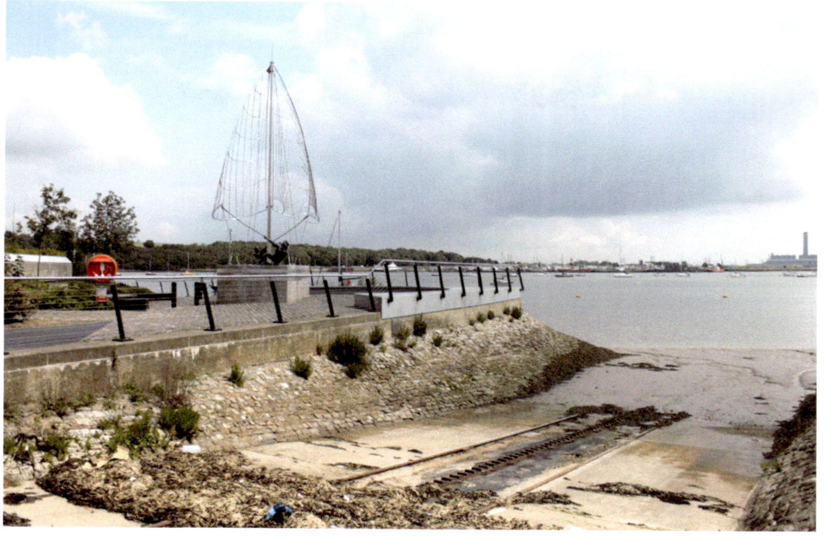

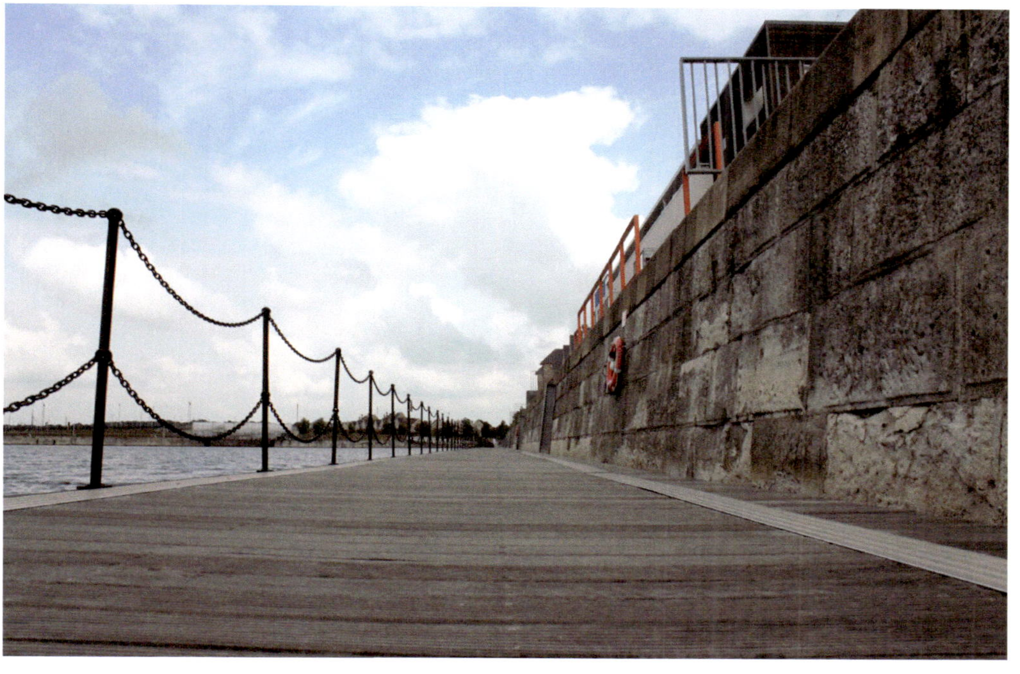

St Mary's as an island was once separated from the mainland by St Mary's Creek. This creek no longer exists, having been transformed during the late nineteenth century into three basins that were to become the centre point of the extended dockyard. Each of these basins was given a specialised role that hinted at a production line process. Once launched, or floated, out of dry dock following underwater repairs to the hull, a vessel would be released into the No. 1 (or repairing) Basin for the completion of work on its upper deck, before being taken to the No. 2 (factory) Basin, as seen in this view, for the installation or repair of machinery and boilers. Finally, the vessel would be moved to the No. 3 (fitting out) Basin for rigging, coaling and the mounting of guns.

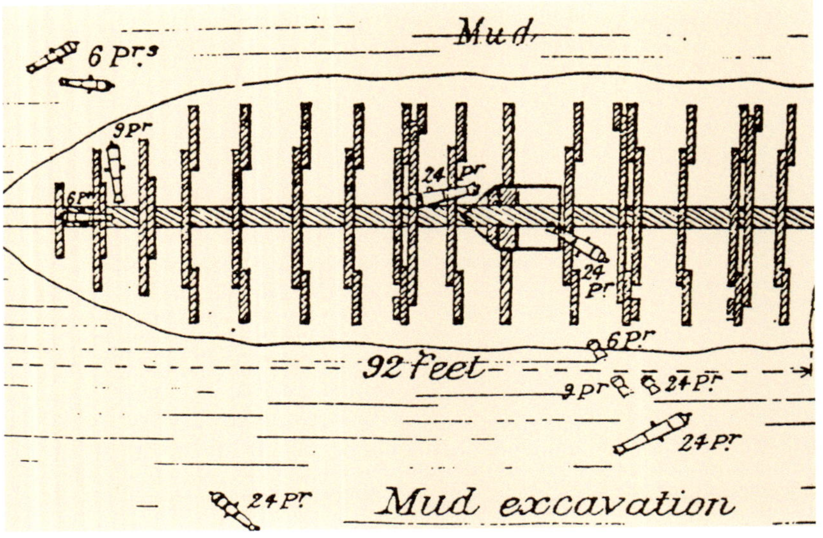

A copy of an 1872 drawing of the remains of a ship discovered in St Mary's Creek while excavation work for the dockyard extension was underway. The ship was possibly *Mathias*, a ship sunk during the Dutch raid on the Medway in 1667.

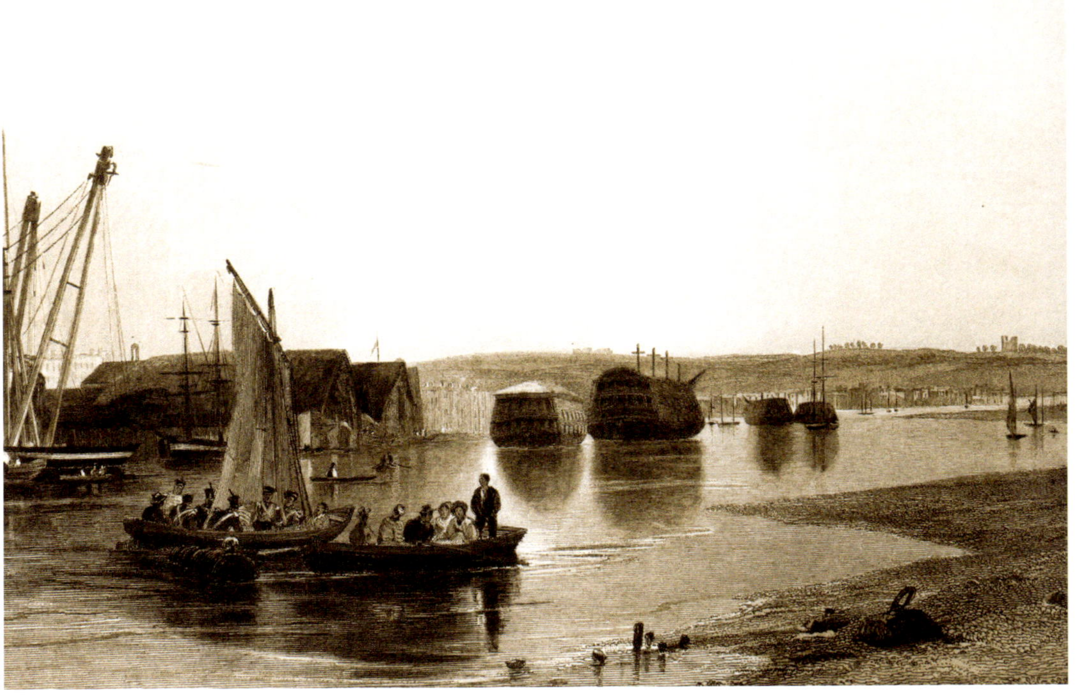

The two boats in the foreground have just run the length of Gillingham Creek and are now approaching the dockyard at Chatham. Whether they are guarding soldiers returning to their barracks or dockyard artisans returning from working on board one of the many moored warships, this early nineteenth-century engraving serves as a reminder that even in the years before the dockyard extension that took the dockyard into the parish of Gillingham, the value of Gillingham to the Navy had once again taken on great significance.

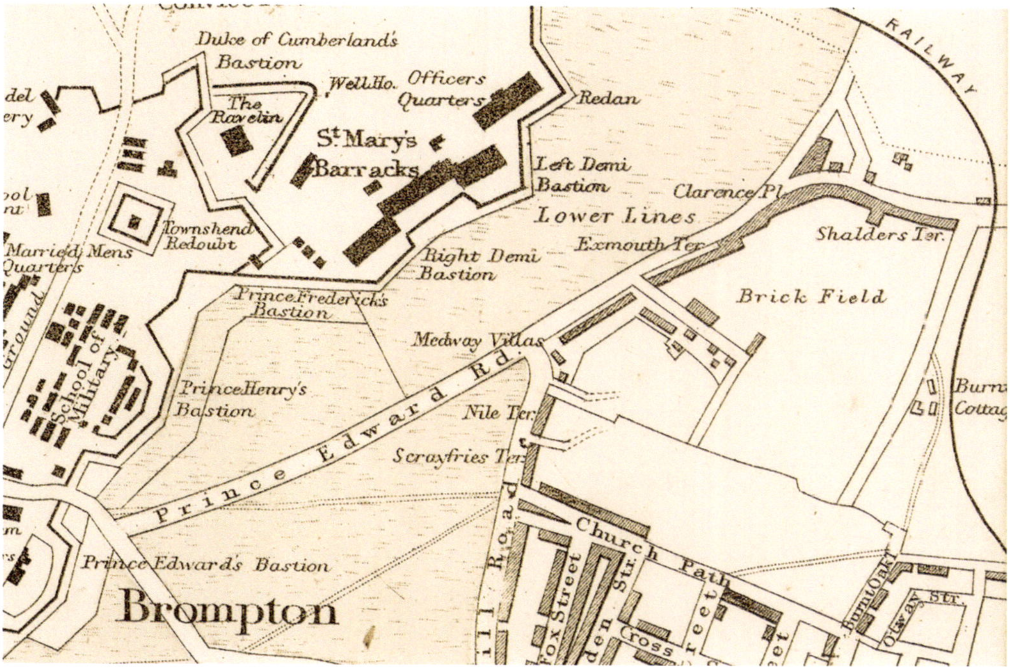

Those who worked in the dockyard at Chatham, due to the proximity of the yard, often sought accommodation within the parish of Gillingham, turning first to Brompton, literally a stone's throw from the dockyard's main gate. But Brompton was only a relatively small enclave, surrounded by land in possession of the military and which was required by the army for mounting a defence of the dockyard should it be attacked by a hostile force. This early eighteenth-century map demonstrates the situation, showing why it became necessary, for the purpose of housing dockyard workers, to develop that area of Gillingham, Britton Farm, which to begin with acquired the name of New Brompton.

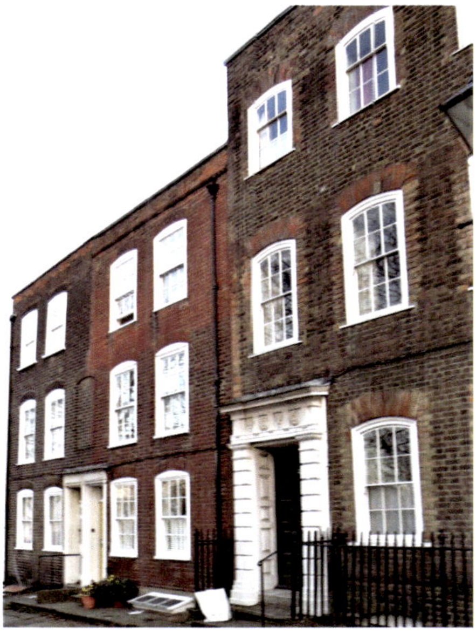

An example of some of the fine Georgian era houses built in Brompton, once home to officers or senior artisans of the dockyard.

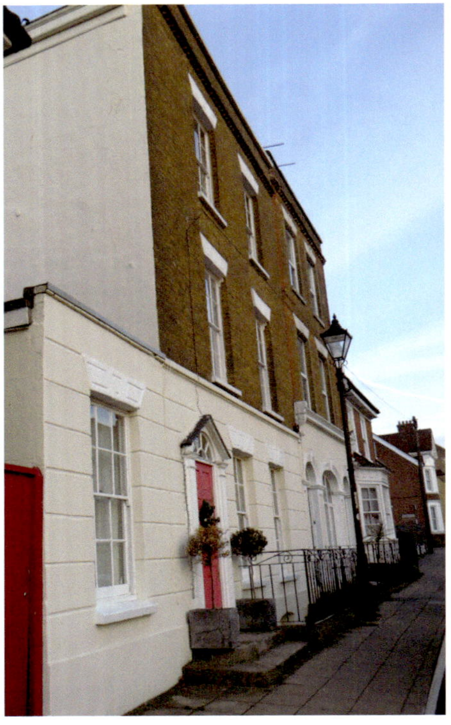

Fine town houses in Brompton were much sought after, an area of Gillingham which even today still possesses a number of very attractive Georgian homes. For the most part these would have accommodated wealthier dockyard artisans, tradespeople or naval officers.

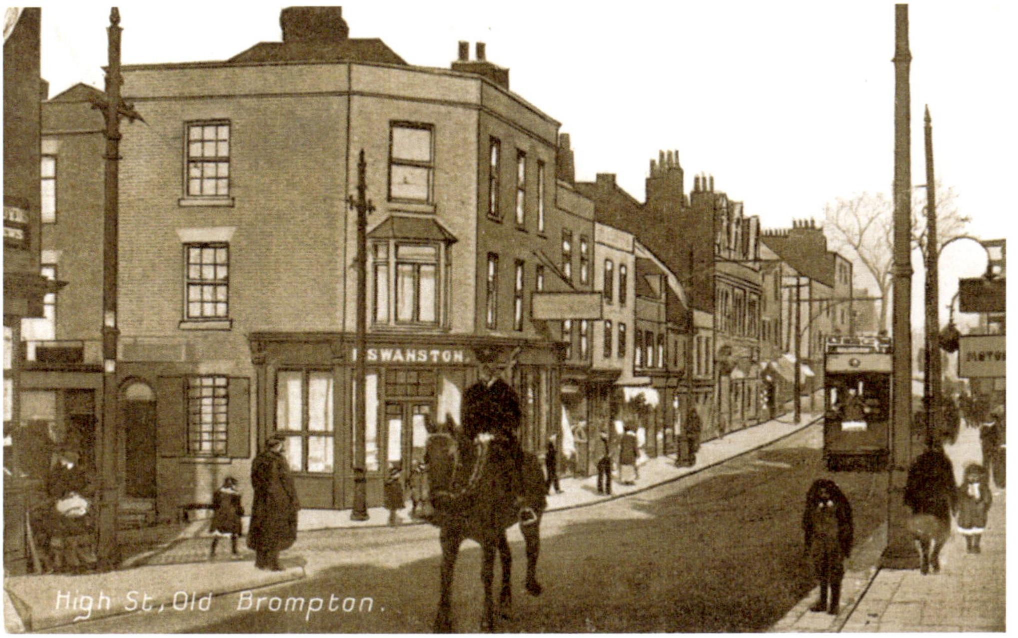

In time, to more helpfully distinguish the Brompton near the yard from New Brompton, the name 'Old Brompton' was adopted. Designated as such in this turn-of-the-century postcard, it fully demonstrates the vibrancy of this dockyard-oriented community.

2

A Military Presence

During the mid-seventeenth century England was frequently at war with the Dutch, while France emerged as the major enemy in later years. Through the Navy, England's first line of defence, the dockyard at Chatham needed to be closely defended, with Gillingham, for this purpose, taking on great importance. In 1667 the Dutch made one near-successful attempt to destroy the dockyard at Chatham. This was recognised as a clear signal that Gillingham, through which enemy forces were likely to pass, needed to be heavily fortified. In mounting their raid on the Medway, a squadron of Dutch ships had reached as far as Gillingham, but were unable to proceed further upriver when brought under fire by the guns of both Upnor Castle and an additional battery hurriedly constructed on the Gillingham side of the river. A chain stretching across the river from Gillingham to the marshy mid-river island of Hoo Ness should also have impeded the progress of the Dutch, but in this it totally failed. Raised by a windlass located on the Gillingham shoreline, the chain was supposed to block the navigable channel, but on reaching the chain the Dutch simply sailed their ships over it. Following the raid, the defences of the river were greatly strengthened, and the dockyard was also eventually secured by construction of the Lines. For Gillingham, the impact was substantial, for apart from new defences built along the shoreline, the military acquired a large slice of land between what was once Old Brompton and New Brompton for construction of the Lines. In turn, those manning these new fortifications required barrack accommodation. Brompton and St Mary's barracks, both in Gillingham, were built for this purpose.

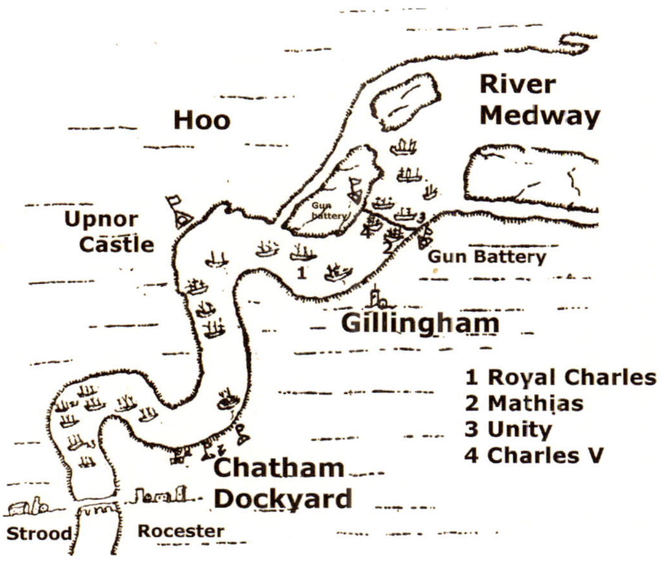

The position of the defences established around Gillingham at the time of the Dutch raid. On the far bank is Upnor Castle, while the Gillingham foreshore possessed a hurriedly constructed gun battery and also served as the anchor point to a chain that, when raised, was intended to block enemy ships making passage upriver. In addition the guard ships *Royal Charles*, *Mathias*, *Unity* and *Charles V* were anchored off Gillingham to protect the river.

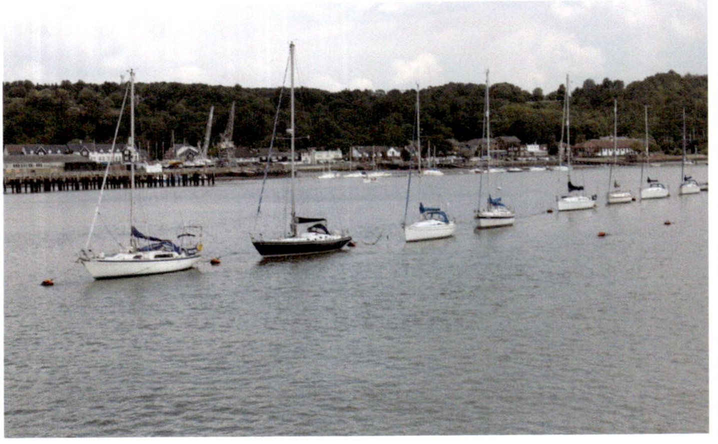

It was here, at this point of the Medway off Gillingham, that the attacking Dutch squadron, mainly through gunfire from Upnor and the battery at Gillingham, was prevented from making further progress upriver.

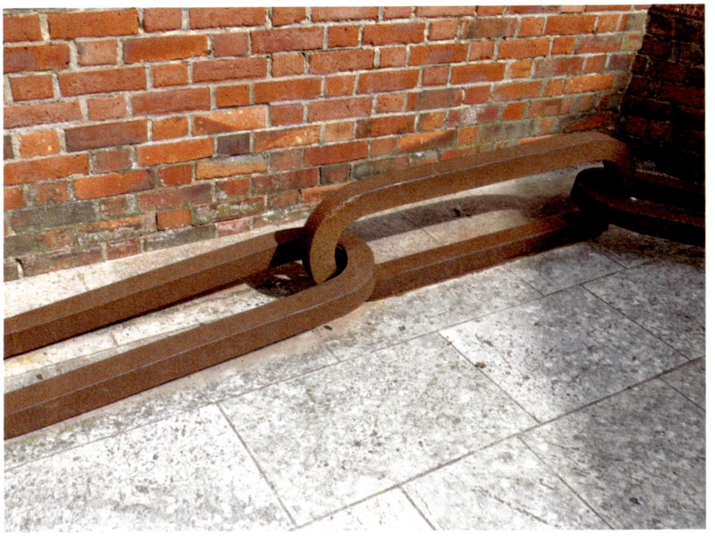

These chain links are a modern-day representation of a chain that once stretched across the harbour at Portsmouth and are probably similar to the chain that once stretched between Gillingham and Hoo Ness. It would have been raised by men hauling on a capstan on the Gillingham side of the river, which slowly drew the chain taut.

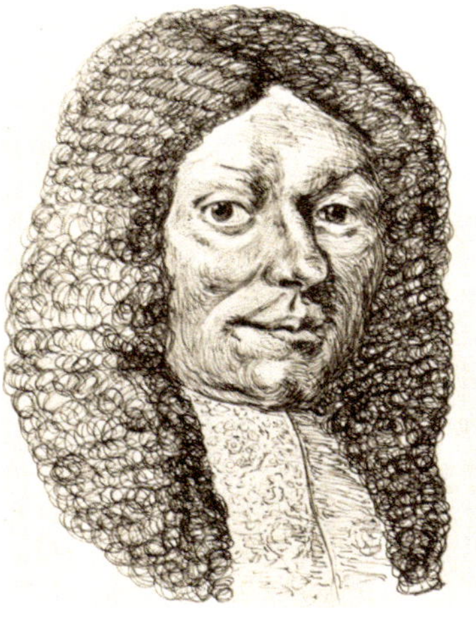

The lesson of the Dutch raid was that the defences of the Medway had to be considerably strengthened, with the area around Gillingham, where a new and better-supported chain was positioned shortly after the raid, needing to be surrounded by permanently positioned gun batteries. The man placed in charge of designing these defences was Bernard de Gomme (1620–83), a military engineer of Flemish descent who had already begun a programme of renewing fortifications in England. The Dutch raid placed a new emphasis on designing fortifications against a second Dutch-style raid.

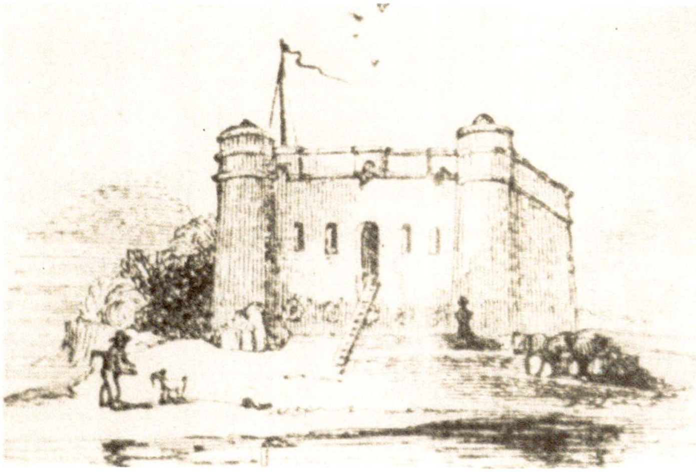

At Gillingham, a fort, as seen in this illustration, was positioned close to the entrance of St Mary's Creek. As constructed, it was a square redoubt, 11 metres (36 feet) in height, and positioned to allow guns on its two faces to fire both up and down stream along the length of Short and Gillingham reaches. By 1698 Gillingham fort was armed with forty culverins and ten demi-culverins.

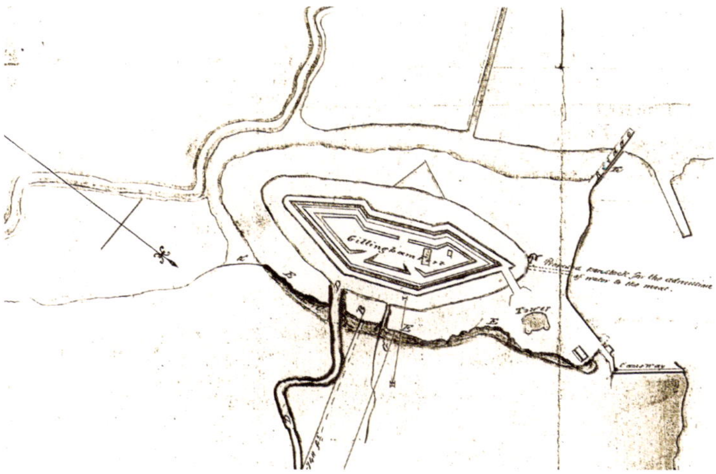

Ground plan of Gillingham Fort showing the position of an additional gun battery that was constructed on the north-east side of the fort.

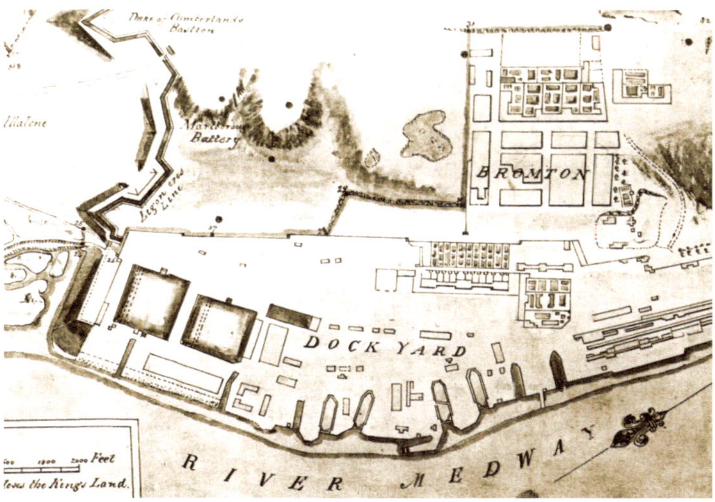

An early eighteenth-century map showing the dockyard (which at that time lay fully outside of Gillingham), as well as the land defences of the dockyard and Brompton, both of which were within the original parish of Gillingham. Known as the Lines, the dockyard land defences were strengthened later in the century and were to be frequently used for the training of troops barracked in Gillingham.

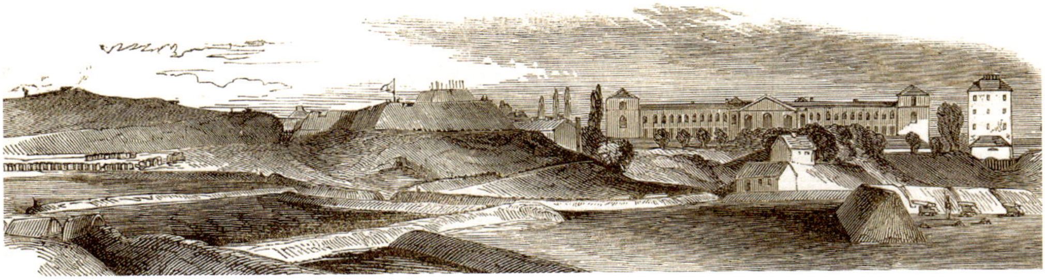

A general view of the Lines, seen here in 1843, looking west, with St Mary's Barracks also to be seen. St Mary's Barracks was built between 1779 and 1782 and occupied by the Army up until 1941 when taken over by the Royal Navy. Demolition of the barracks took place during the early 1960s.

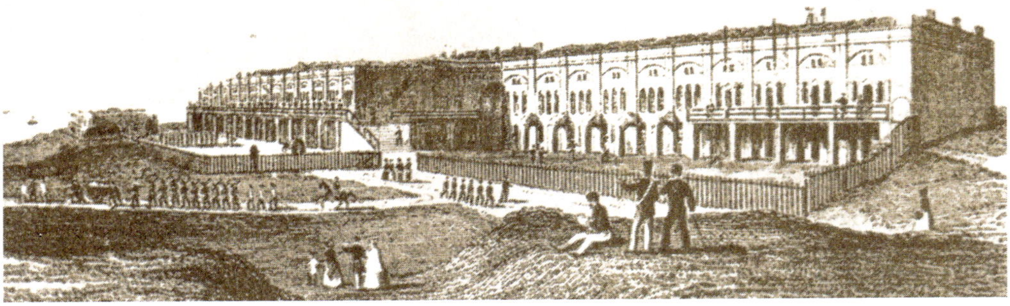

St Mary's Barracks, seen here during the early part of the nineteenth century. As with Brompton Barracks, but prior to acquisition by the Royal Navy, St Mary's had been gradually acquired by the Corps of Royal Engineers. In 1816 the barracks were used for storage and later, during the Crimean War, as a military hospital.

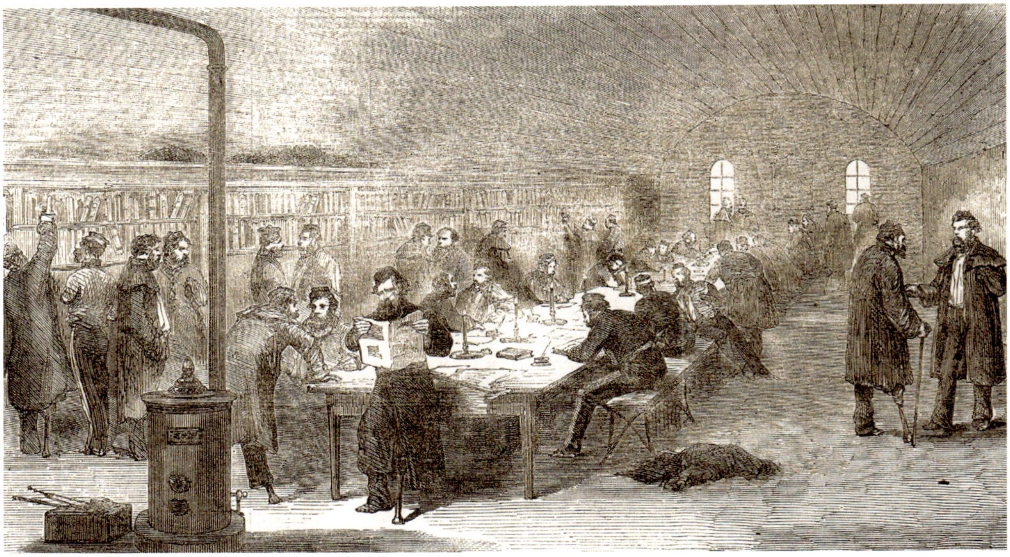

St Mary's Barracks reading room seen here in 1856 when in use as a military hospital.

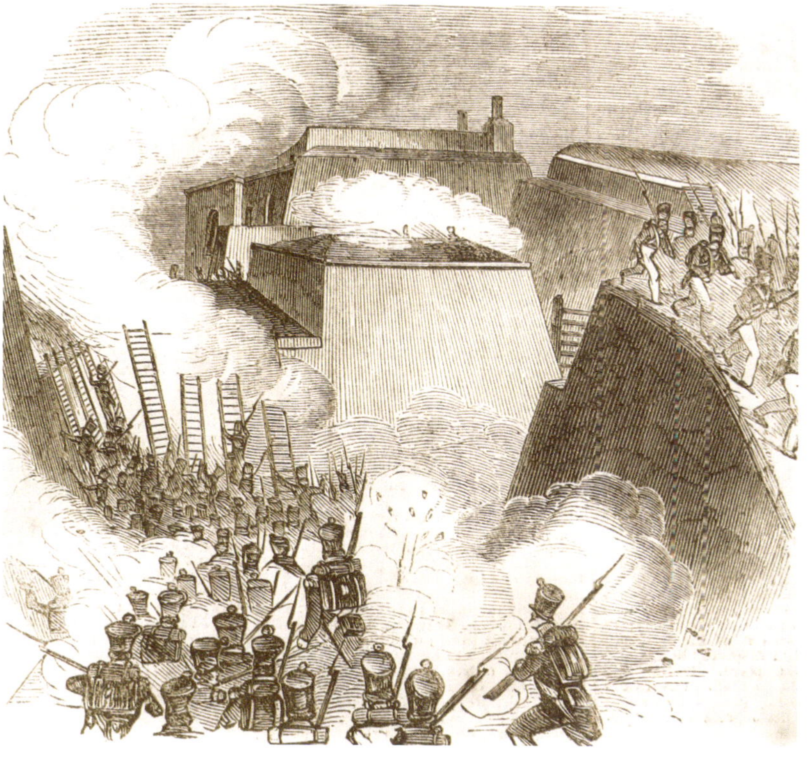

The Lines were frequently used for military exercises, usually involving many hundreds of soldiers drawn from the surrounding area, including Brompton and St Mary's Barracks. Here, during the late summer of 1843, the Outer Lines overlooking St Mary's Island is under attack by one portion of troops while another acts as defenders.

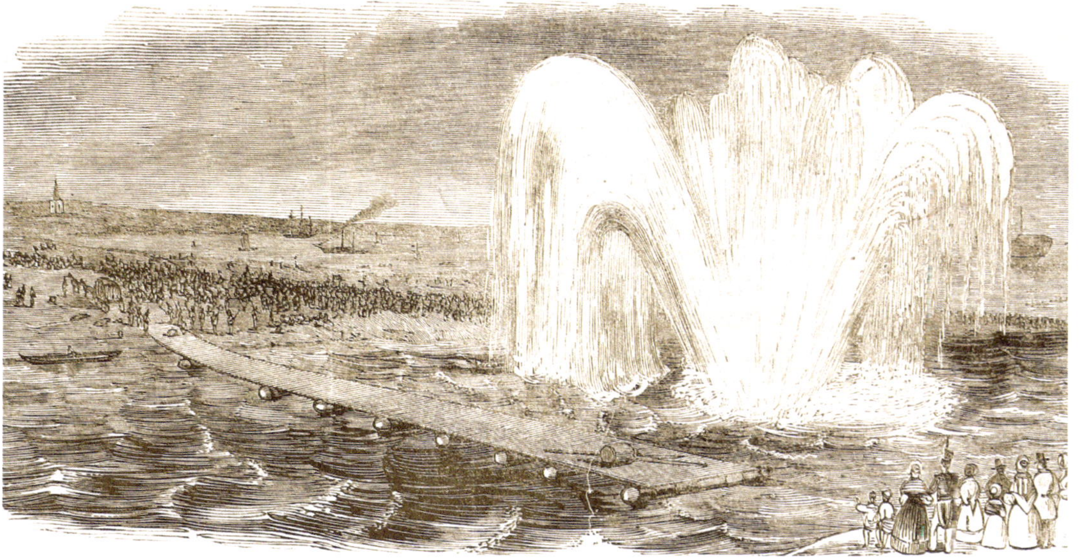

As part of the military exercise undertaken during the late summer of 1843, a pontoon bridge was laid across St Mary's Creek by the Royal Engineers. However, the work on this occasion was left unfinished due to it being crashed into by a barge. Coupled with the assembly of the pontoon bridge was an experiment to gauge the effectiveness of various underwater explosives. A rock, long considered a hazard to navigation, was successfully destroyed, with the explosion visible in this contemporary print.

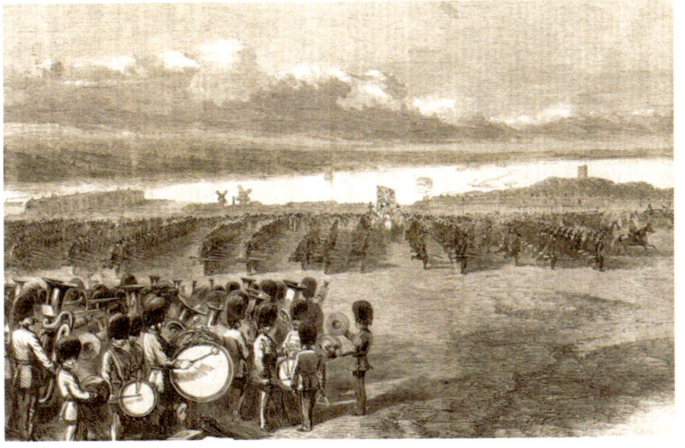

Military exercises on the Lines drew in crowds from far and wide. Spectators, usually from a safe distance, were allowed to view the various attack and defence manoeuvres. Adding to such occasions was the presence of military bands playing soldierly music.

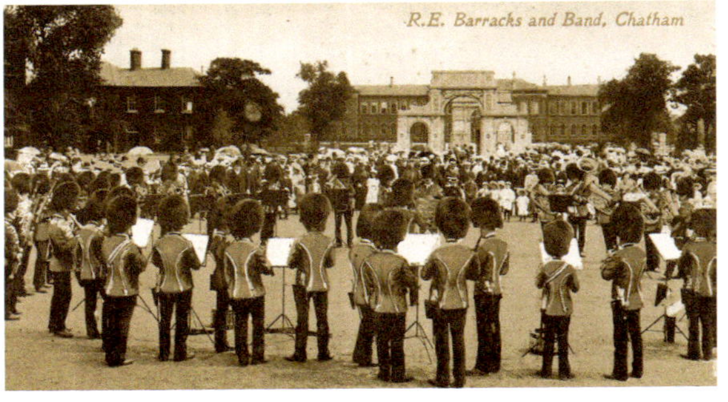

Brompton Barracks, just outside the original area of the Lines, still serves the needs of the Corps of Royal Engineers. The parade ground is seen here in this early twentieth-century postcard view.

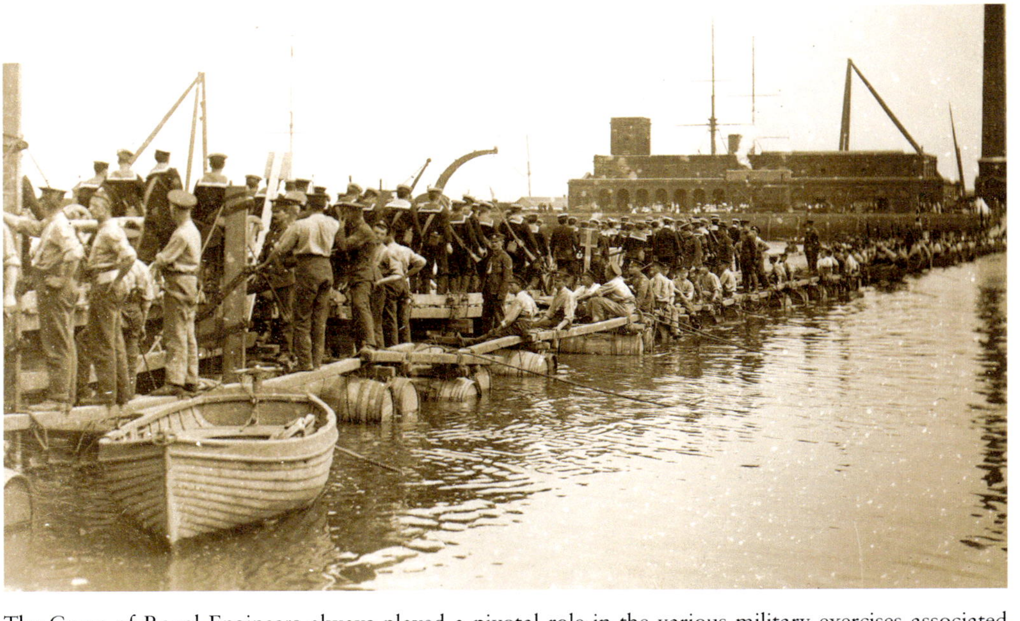

The Corps of Royal Engineers always played a pivotal role in the various military exercises associated with the Lines. One particular specialism of the Royal Engineers usually called upon was the construction of pontoon bridges such as the one depicted earlier and built across St Mary's Creek. By contrast, the bridge seen here dates to the early twentieth century and crosses the River Medway to reach the dockyard extension that had been built on St Mary's Island.

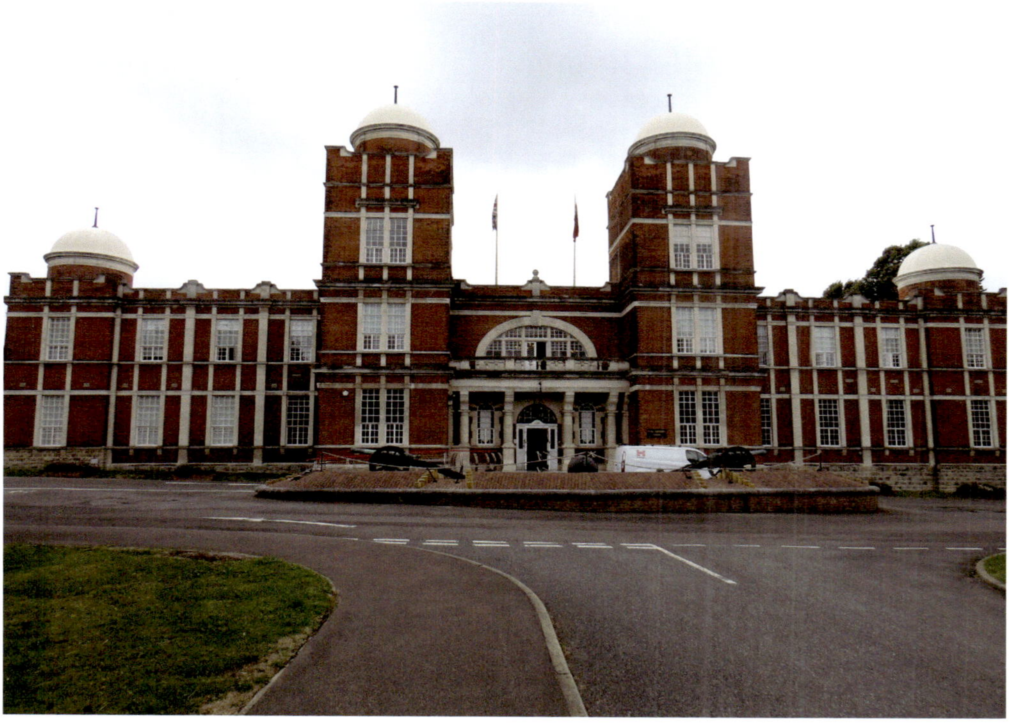

Located on Prince Arthur Road, this building, which now serves as the Royal Engineers Museum, was first opened in 1905 as the Electrical School of the Corps of Royal Engineers. Since 1987, when it was officially opened by Her Majesty the Queen on 20 May of that year, the building has served as the Corps Museum. The Royal Engineers Museum had originally been established in 1912, at that time located in the North Block of Brompton Barracks. In time, space available became far too limited for the housing of a major collection of artefacts, leading to the later move to the former Electrical School.

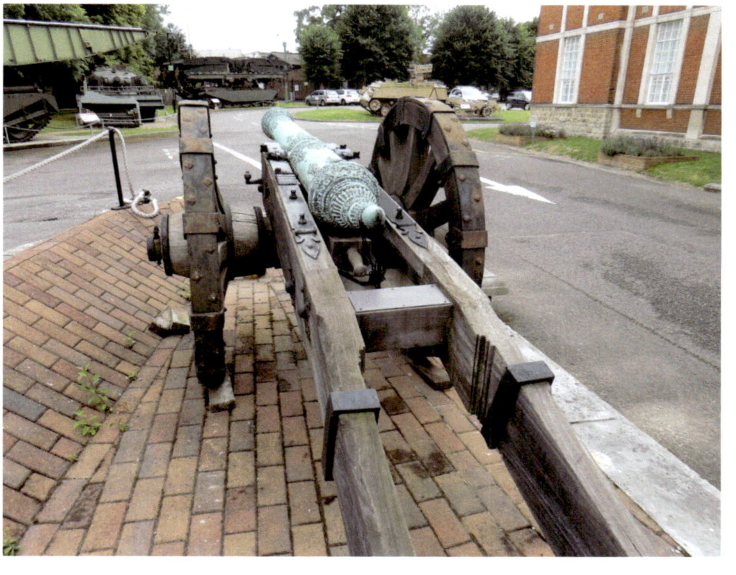

Displayed outside the Royal Engineers Museum, this brass cannon was captured at Mandalay on 28 November 1885. At the time Mandalay was Burma's royal capital city, with the British annexing the kingdom on that day. In general it was a bad day for Mandalay, a group of drunken British soldiers later that same day setting fire to the Royal Library, which contained the kingdom's official records.

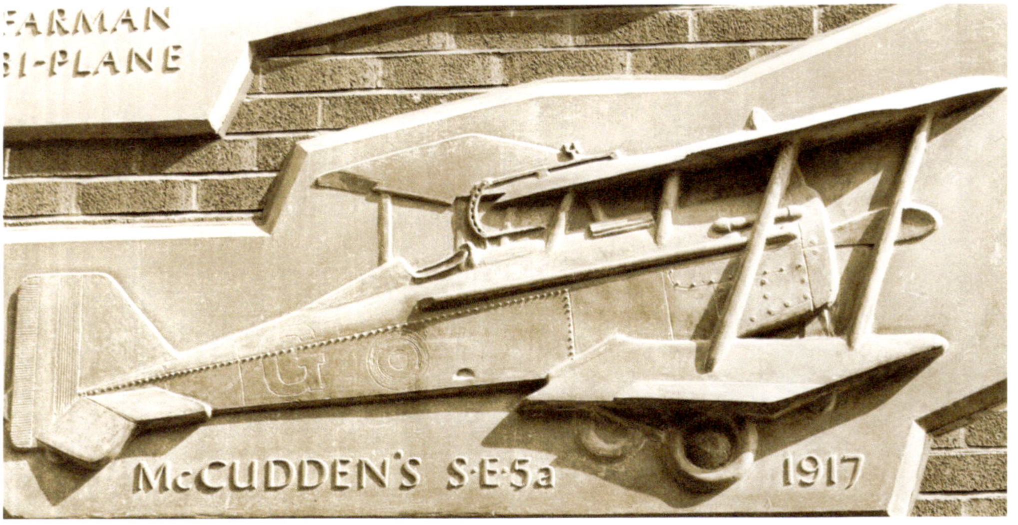

One of Gillingham's most famous wartime heroes was First World War flying ace James Thomas Byford McCudden VC. He was born in the town on 22 March 1895. Following in his father's footsteps, McCudden joined the Royal Engineers, serving as a bugler for three years. However, in April 1913 he transferred to the Royal Flying Corps (RFC), seeing flight as a thing of the future.

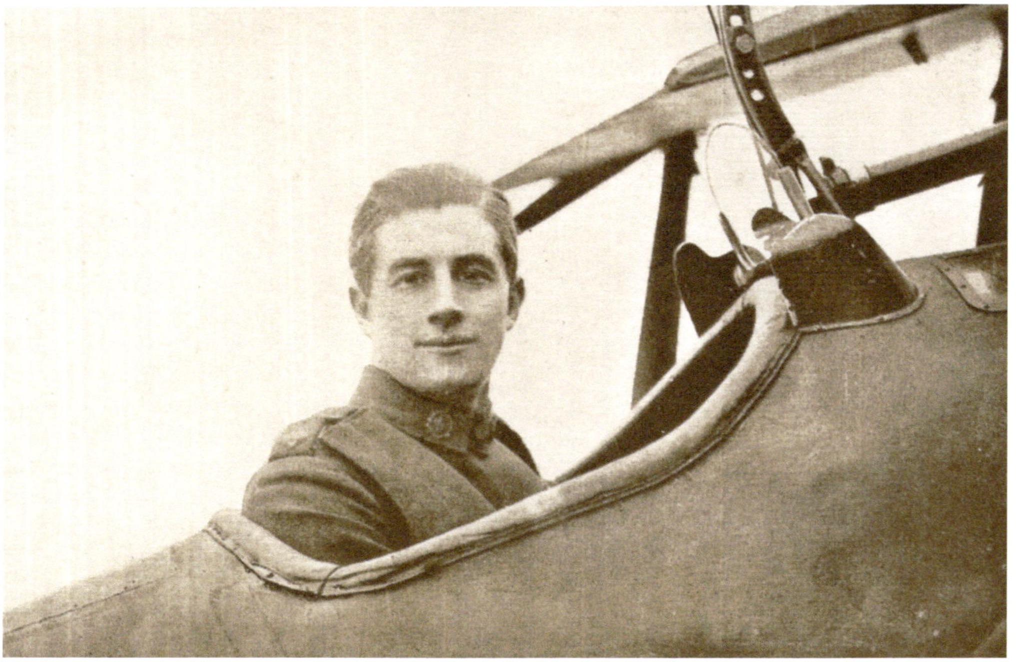

James McCudden seated in the cockpit of his SE5 biplane fighter. McCudden did not survive the war; he was killed on 9 July 1918, aged twenty-three, when his aeroplane crashed shortly after take-off from an airfield in Auxi-le-Château in France.

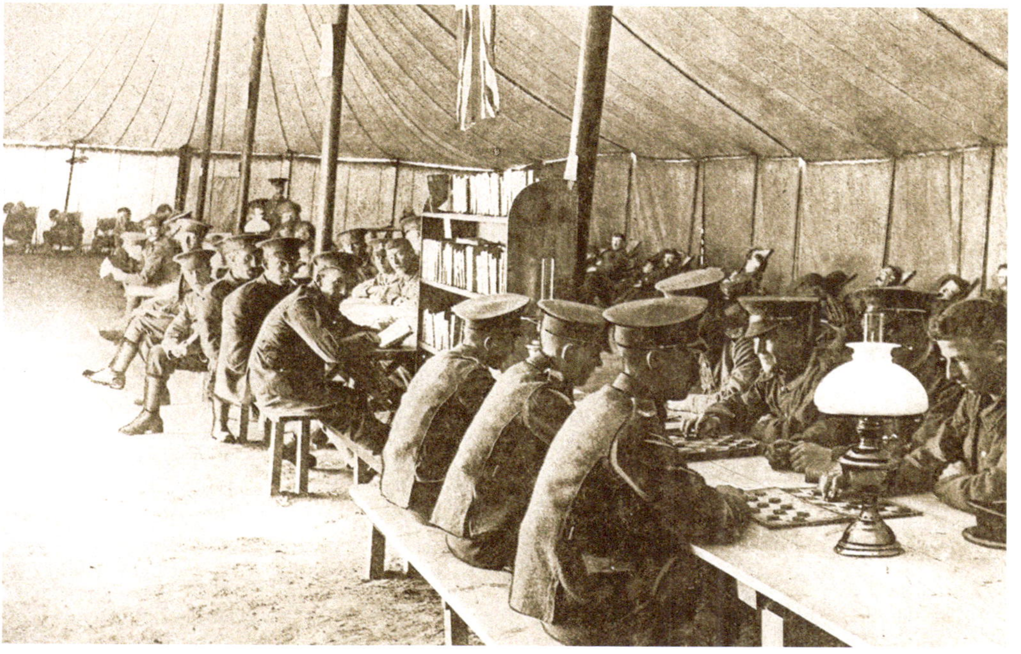

During the twentieth century the Lines continued to be used for training exercises by troops who might one day be called on to defend the dockyard from attack. Here, soldiers on exercise in Gillingham spend their recreational time in makeshift tents, as the barracks and other military facilities in the area were unable to accommodate those undergoing summer training.

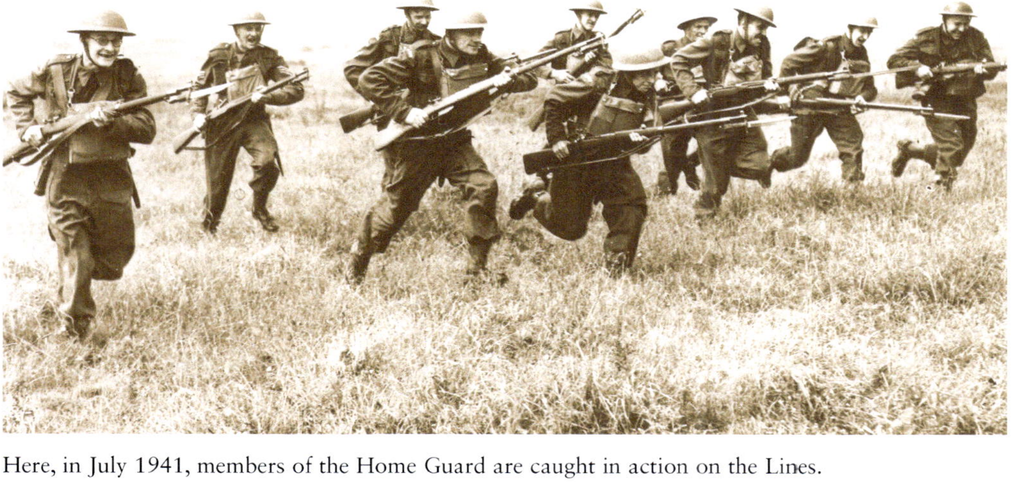

Here, in July 1941, members of the Home Guard are caught in action on the Lines.

3

Prisons and Prison Ships

A frequently overlooked aspect of Gillingham's lost past is its use as an area for the holding of prisoners, sometimes prisoners of war but at other times convicted felons. During the many wars fought during the eighteenth century and on into the time of Napoleon Bonaparte, the success of the British Navy in capturing enemy ships saw the crews of many of those ships brought to the Medway off Gillingham, where they would be incarcerated on long out of service warships known as hulks. Sometimes convicts were also held on such hastily converted warships because a sentence of 'hard labour' could mean employment in the naval dockyard at Chatham. The extension of the dockyard, all of which was built in Gillingham during the reign of Queen Victoria, also initially relied heavily on convict labour, leading to the building of a large prison on St Mary's Island.

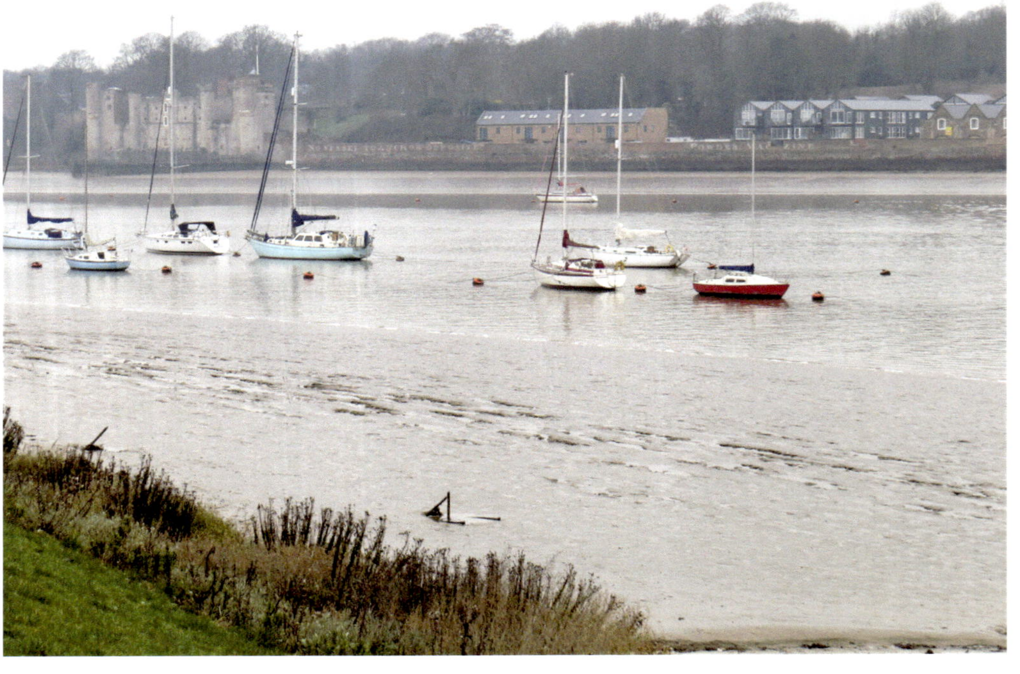

A stretch of the River Medway off Gillingham would have, during the eighteenth century, been home to a number of ageing warships, some of them converted into prison ships to hold either prisoners of war or convicts.

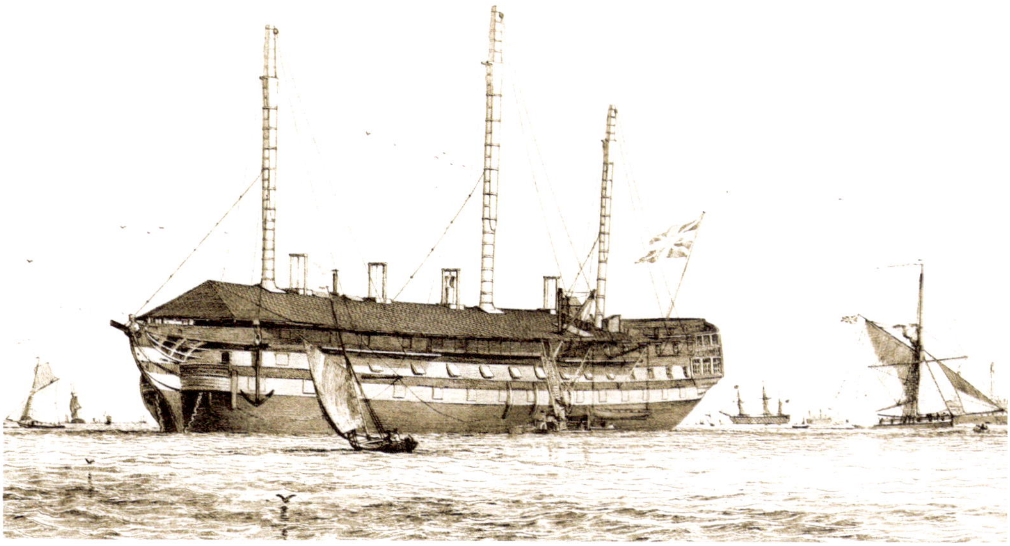

An impression of what these hulks looked like can be gained from this drawing, first published in 1829, of the seventy-four-gun warship *Hastings* lying in the Medway off Gillingham. It was never converted into a prison hulk but did end its career many years later as a coal hulk.

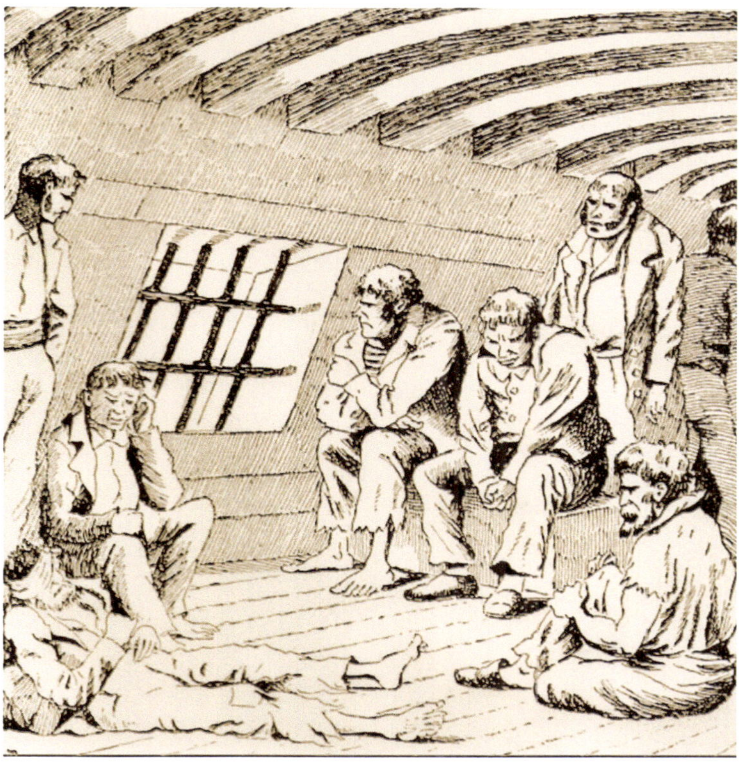

Life on board a prison hulk, as depicted here, was far from pleasant. Those incarcerated lived together on the crowded, unventilated lower decks, leading to the frequent outbreak of diseases such as typhus. Many died on board, their bodies unceremoniously buried in the marshes on St Mary's Island.

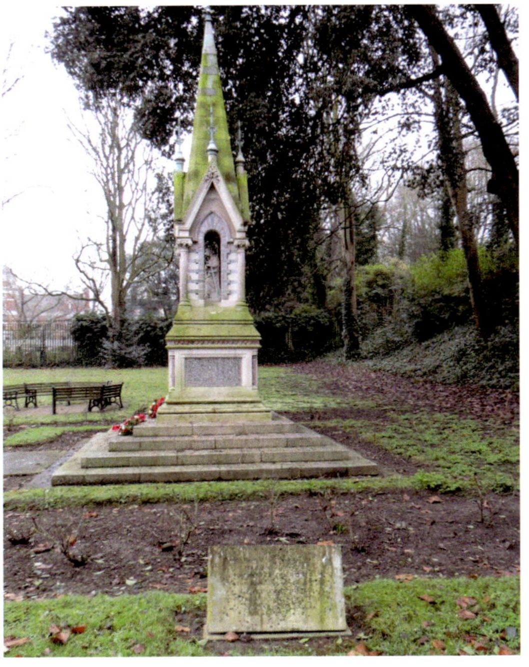

In time, the burial site of those French seamen who had died in captivity became known as the French cemetery on St Mary's Island, with additional skeletons later brought there from other known sites where French prisoners of war had been locally buried. In 1869 a striking monument, as seen here, was erected in the centre of French cemetery, with the Admiralty allotting a small sum annually for its upkeep. The work of actually erecting the monument was carried out by some of the convict labour previously assigned to constructing the new dockyard extension.

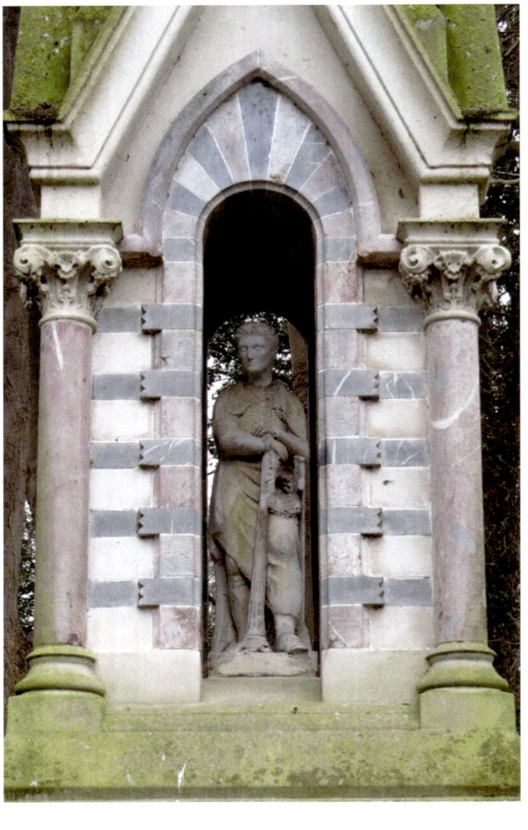

Detail of the memorial to the French prisoners. In design, the plinth and steps were granite, while finely carved figures are displayed under a canopied and groined spire. In 1904 it became necessary to move the bones of the prisoners of war and in that year they were interred in the grounds of the new naval barracks, a site having been set apart for the purpose near the chapel. Here the monument was re-erected, occupying a position where it could easily be seen by onlookers. Initially some 506 skulls were moved, although later, *c.* 1910, two further skeletons were discovered during excavation work for a new wharf close by the Strand, where the gasworks was later established.

William Burnett, a naval surgeon who later rose to become the Royal Navy's chief physician, during the early winter of 1814, was charged with overseeing the care arrangements for all seamen in the River Medway including prisoners held on board the hulks moored off Gillingham. During that time Burnett, ignoring all risk to his own health, successfully brought an end to a typhoid fever epidemic that, prior to his arrival, had claimed the lives of several hundred prisoners. More on Burnett while overseeing naval medical arrangements in the Medway can be found in *Secret Chatham*, a companion volume to *Secret Gillingham*.

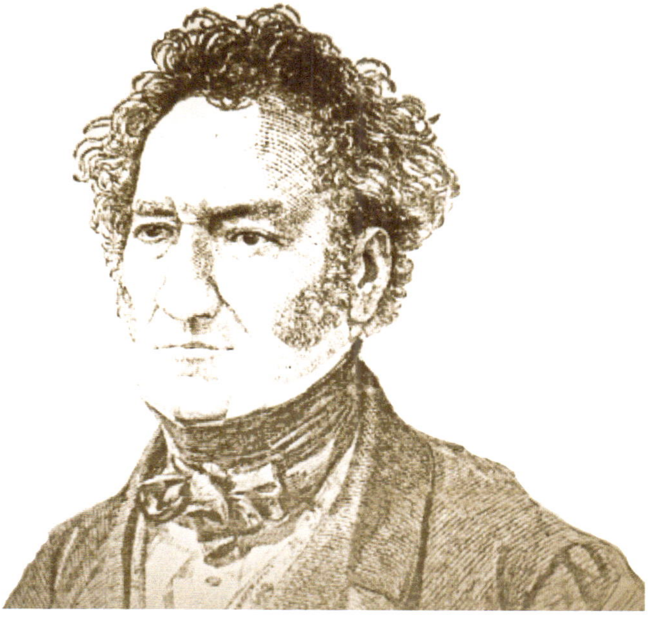

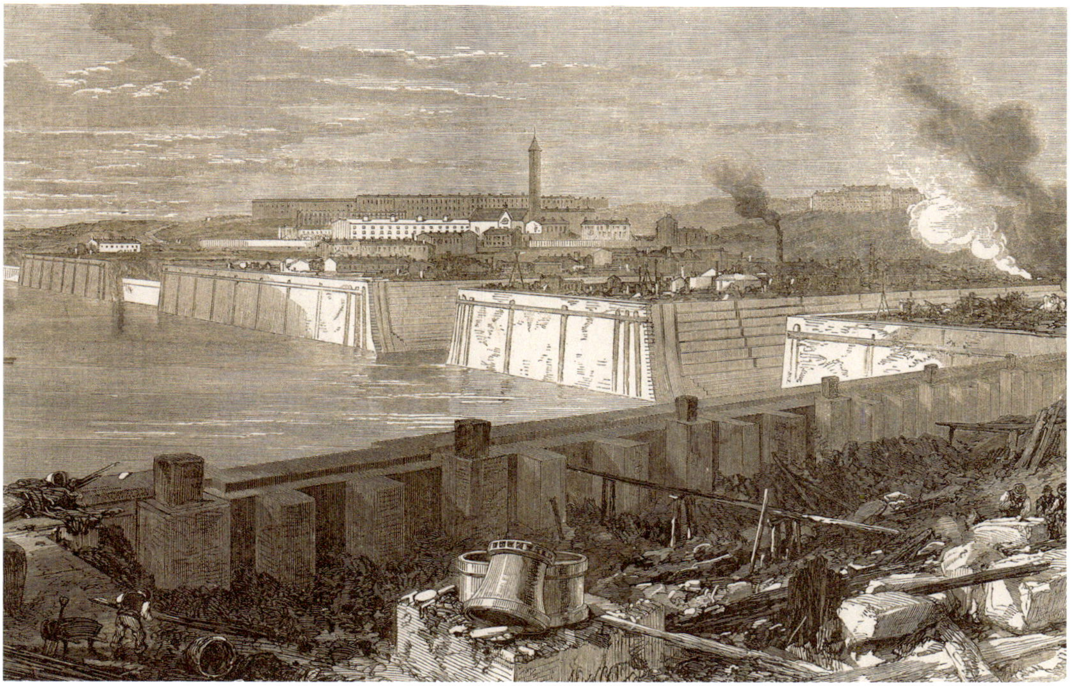

Before work could begin on the large-scale extension to the naval dockyard that was begun during the 1860s, with much of the initial work carried out by convicts, those convicts had first to be employed in the construction of a prison that would house them, together with construction of a masonry wall to surround St Mary's Island to prevent it being flooded. Here, in the distance, is a view of the prison with convicts at work in the foreground on one of the basins.

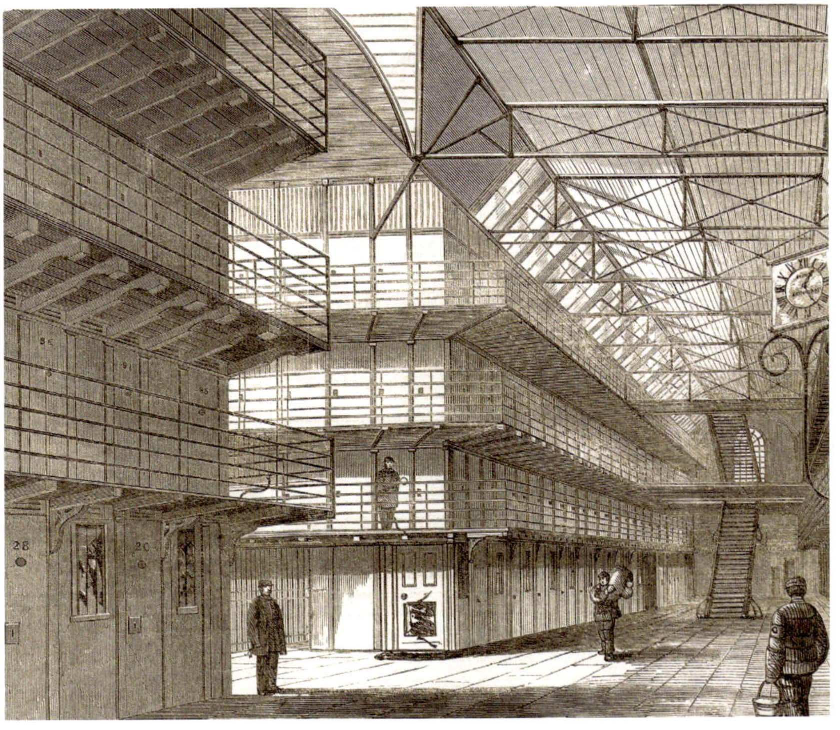

An interior view of St Mary's Island prison.

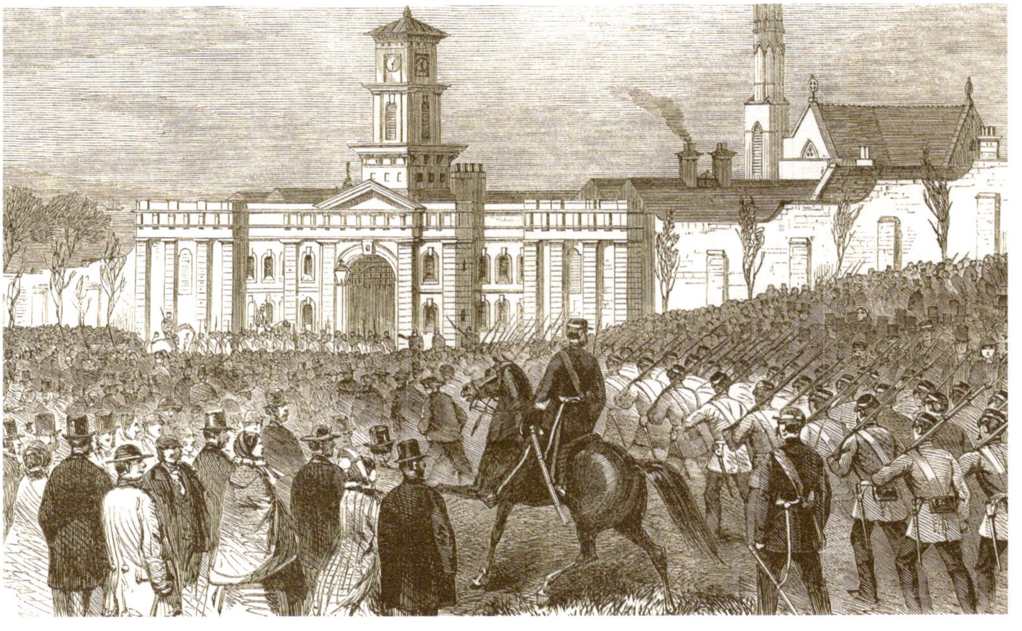

Forced to work long hours and treated inhumanely by the wardens, resentment among the convicts held at the prison was considerable. In February 1861 a full-scale riot broke out, resulting in partial destruction of the prison by the inmates. To quell the situation a large body of troops was detailed to put down the riot.

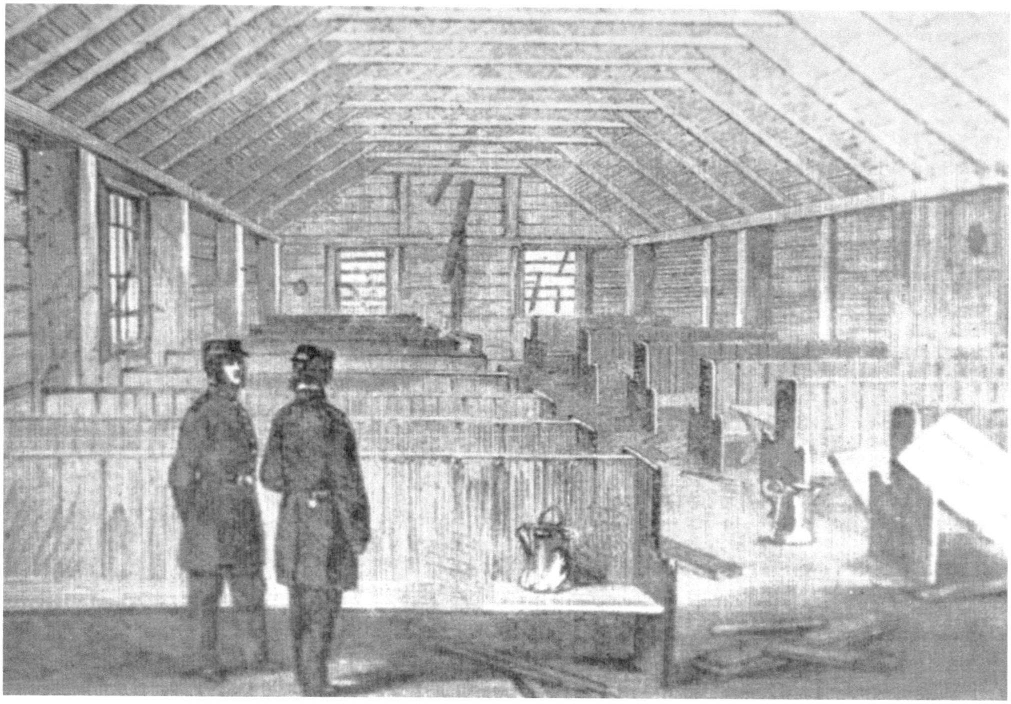

Warders from the St Mary's Island prison seen here inspecting damage to the canteen following the riot. It was here, in the canteen, that the first outward sign of trouble was witnessed; the prisoners, in rejecting the cold and tasteless soup that they were given, threw the contents of their soup bowls at the Chief Warden. It took some four hours for order to be restored, but a few days later an even more serious riot broke out.

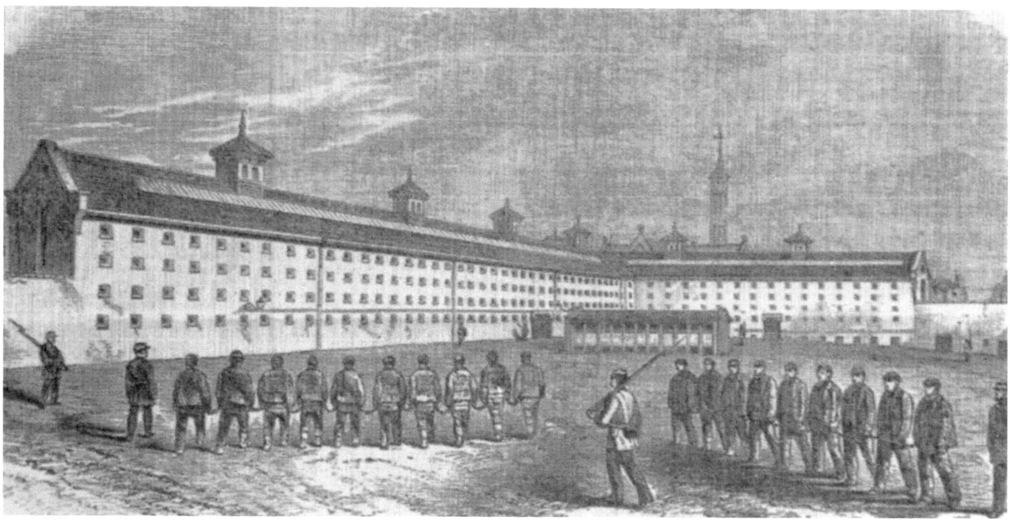

The prison parade ground with armed soldiers seen escorting a number of manacled convicts following the riots. As punishment, many of the prisoners remained chained and locked in their cells for a week, while a further forty or more were whipped.

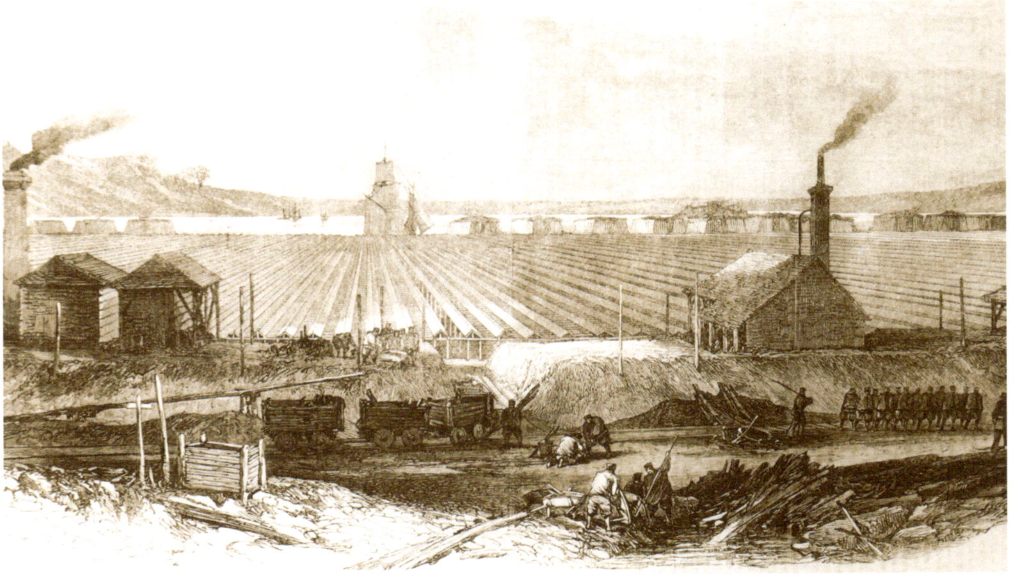

One particular task assigned to the convicts was working the brickfield on St Mary's Island, as seen here in an *Illustrated London News* engraving of April 1867. In total, more than 110 million bricks were produced, with the convicts having first drained and levelled a 21-acre site of marshland before installing six brick-making machines that had been supplied by the Atlas Works of London.

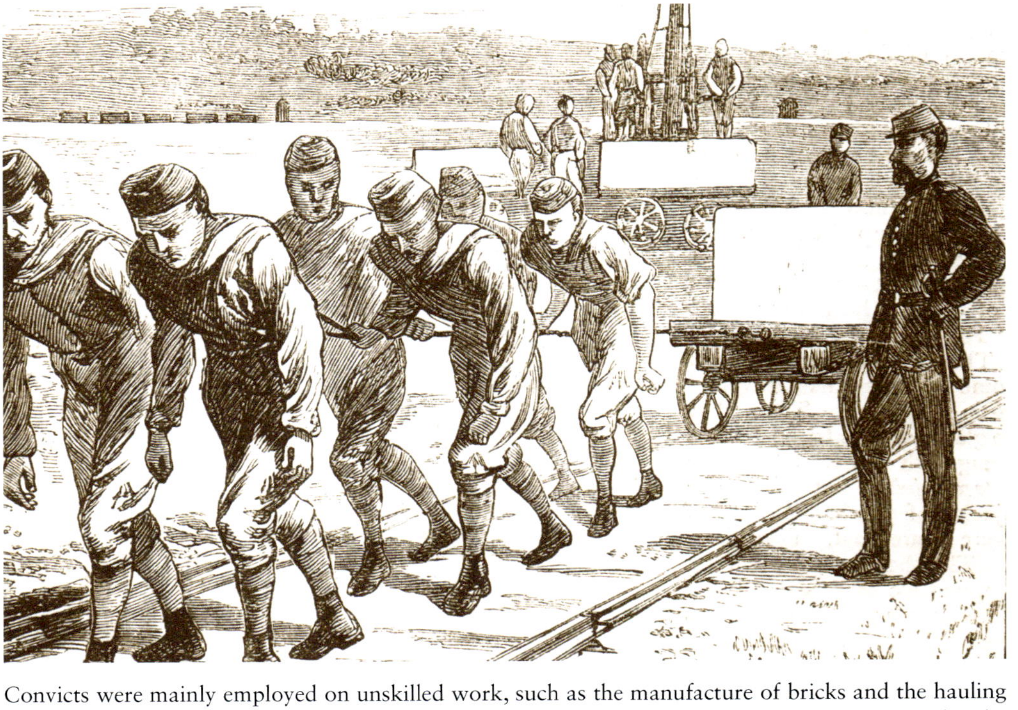

Convicts were mainly employed on unskilled work, such as the manufacture of bricks and the hauling of loads from one part of the construction site to another. Of course, they were always under the watchful gaze of a prison warden.

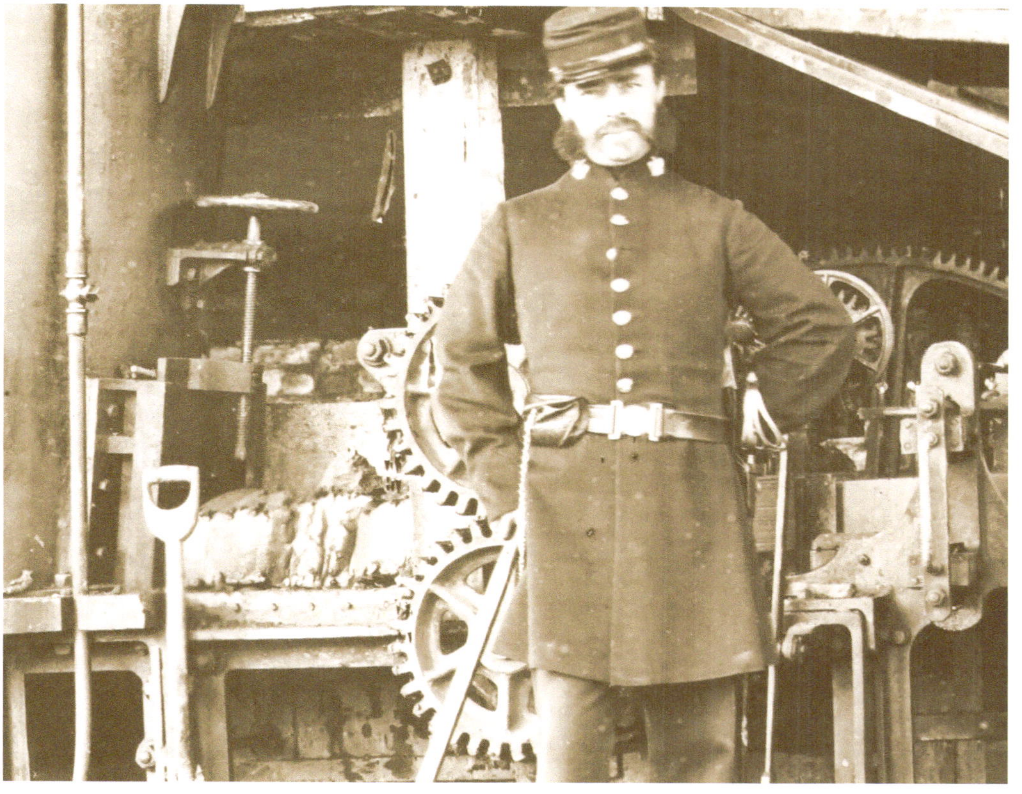

One of the prison wardens.

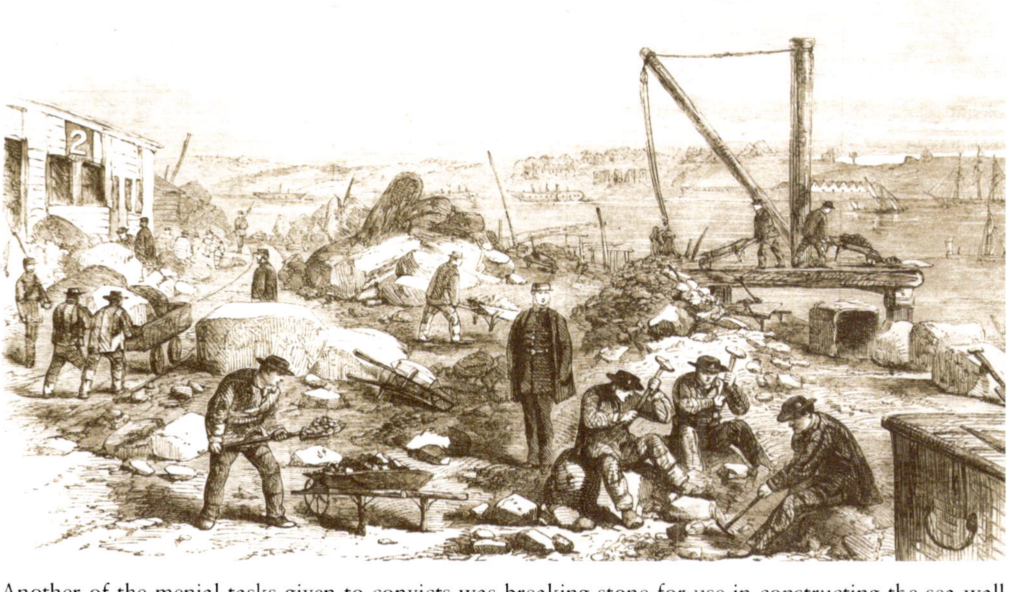

Another of the menial tasks given to convicts was breaking stone for use in constructing the sea wall and the sides of the three giant basins that were the centre-part of the dockyard extension.

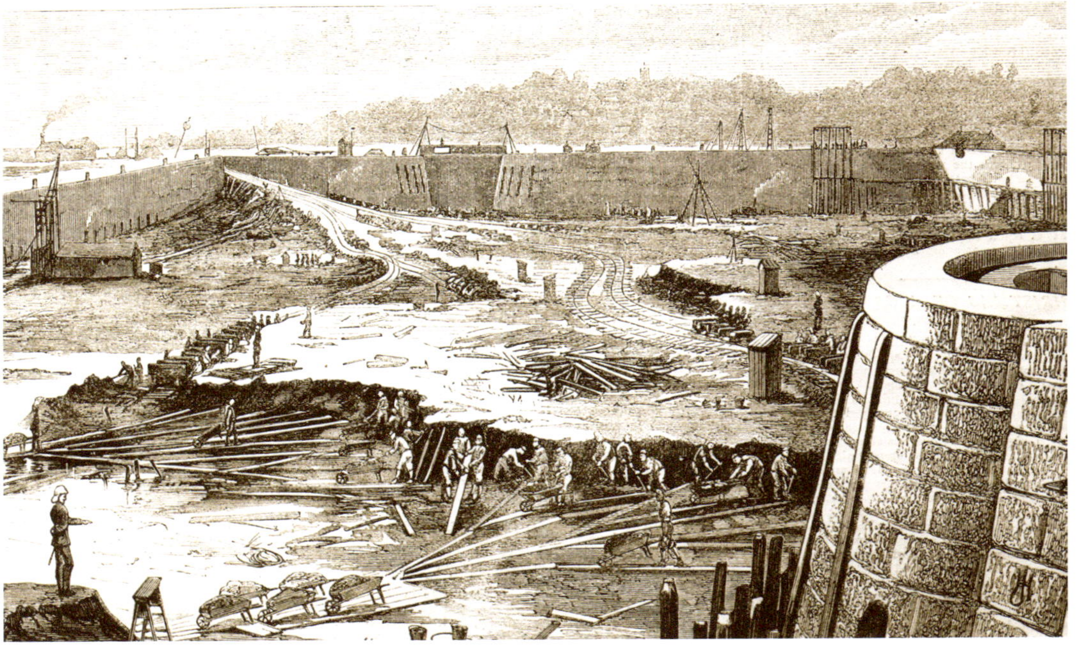

Still under the watchful gaze of the prison wardens, convicts here are employed on laying the future No. 1 Basin.

4

A Victorian Dockyard

One event more than any other was responsible for the creation of modern-day Gillingham, turning it from a semi-rural parish with a population centred primarily on 'Old Brompton' while elsewhere much of the parish consisted of farmland and open countryside. This one single event was an Admiralty decision to construct the iron-hulled battleship *Achilles* within the dockyard at Chatham. It was the first such ship to be launched in a royal dockyard, with many others soon to follow. This move from constructing ships of timber to constructing ships of iron required not just a massive increase in the total workforce employed and a change in the skills required of that workforce but a considerable increase in the facilities of the yard. This, in turn, led to a massive extension to the yard – an extension built entirely within the parish of Gillingham. Indeed, by the 1870s, much more of Chatham dockyard lay within Gillingham rather than Chatham, but with the yard retaining its original name. As for the effect on Gillingham, it now became an even more essential settlement hub, providing the vast majority of this new and constantly expanding workforce with space for homes and various recreational facilities.

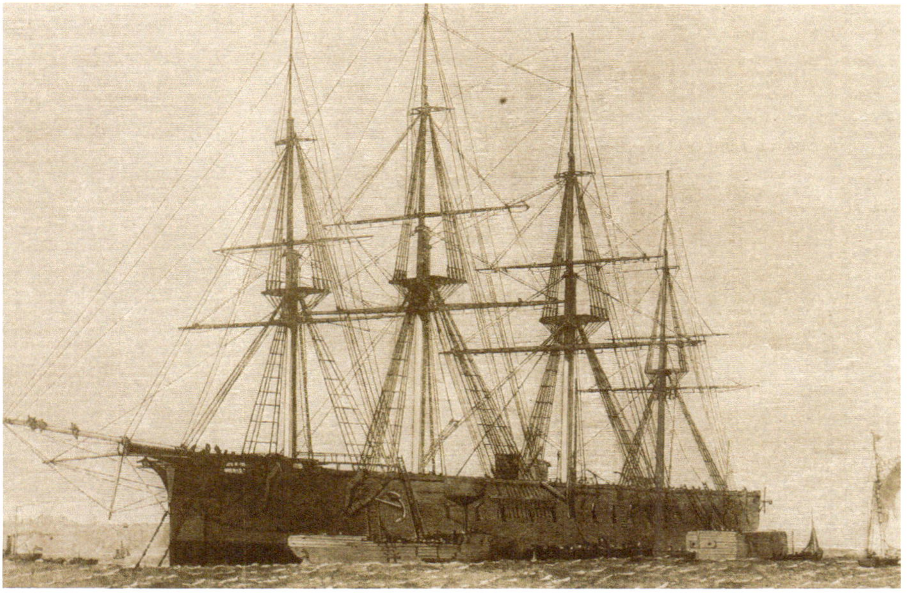

Achilles, the ship that transformed Gillingham into a large-scale built-up municipality, the first true iron-hulled battleship to be launched in a royal dockyard, seen here moored off Gillingham where she is in the final stages of being fitted out for sea. Constructed in the No. 2 dock (rather than upon a building slip), *Achilles* was floated into the Medway in December 1863 and commissioned for service in the Channel Squadron nine months later.

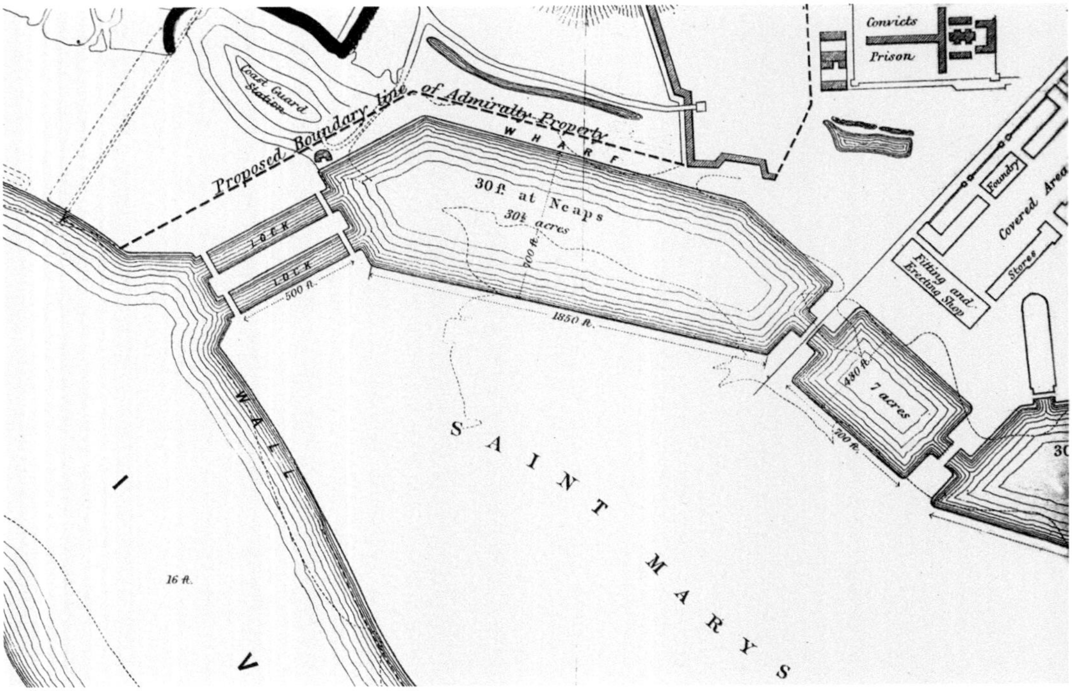

The area of the subsequently completed extension was first marked out in December 1860, with the cost of completing the necessary river wall and embankment estimated at £902,000. An enabling Act was passed in July 1861 and convicts were soon undertaking excavation work on the area designated for the basins. While the concept for the extension remained unchanged, the design and layout of the three basins was to see various alterations. This plan, dating to the late 1850s, shows how they were to be originally laid out.

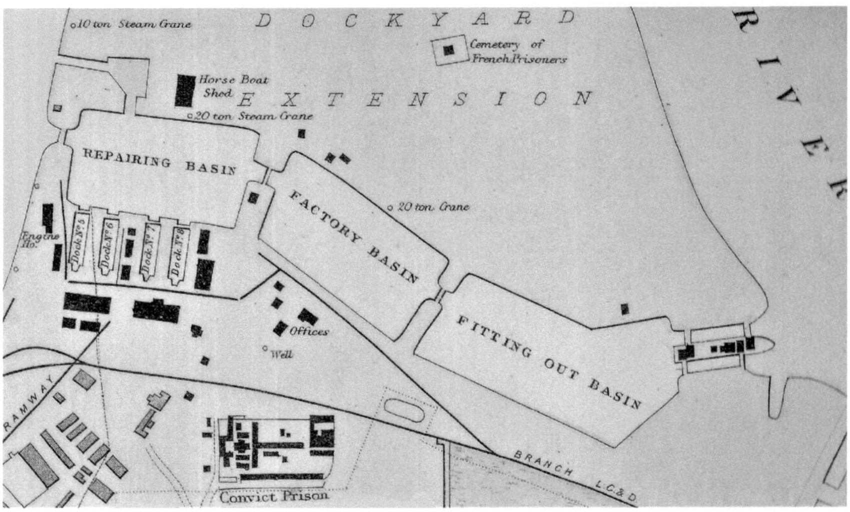

The extension was finally completed by the late 1870s, and the basins now take on a more orderly layout. A particular feature of the extension was the taking in of St Mary's Island in its entirety, leaving further areas where later buildings could be added as and when required.

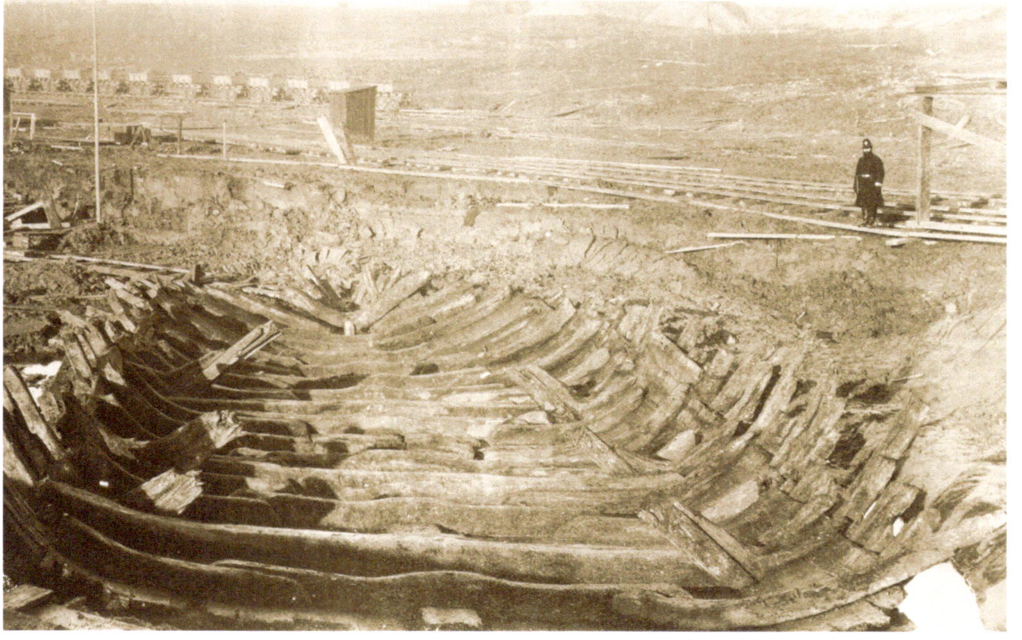

During construction of the basins, a discovery was made of a ship burnt to the waterline that dates to the Dutch raid of 1667. In this day and age the timbers as discovered would have been carefully removed, dried out over a lengthy period of time and then placed on display in a purpose-built museum. Instead, the remains of the ship were simply photographed and drawings made, with the vessel left in position and the remains, presumably, still somewhere under the foundations of No. 1 (fitting out) Basin. A copy of the drawing as made at the time can be seen on page 16.

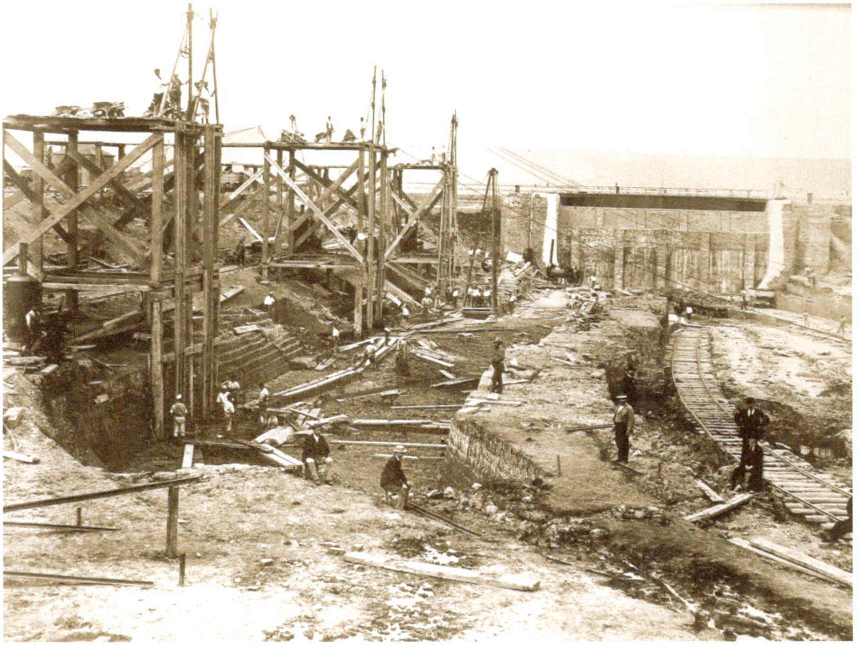

Construction work under way on the Repairing Basin.

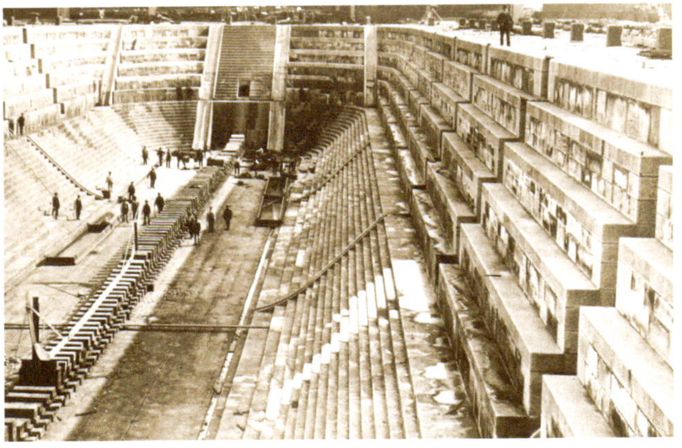

Seen here *c*.1870 and close to completion, No. 5 Dock was the first of four docks on the south side of the Repairing (No. 1) Basin. As with those other three docks, No. 5 Dock had a length of 420 feet with a depth of 28 feet 6 inches over the sill at high water neaps, and 31 feet 6 inches at high water springs.

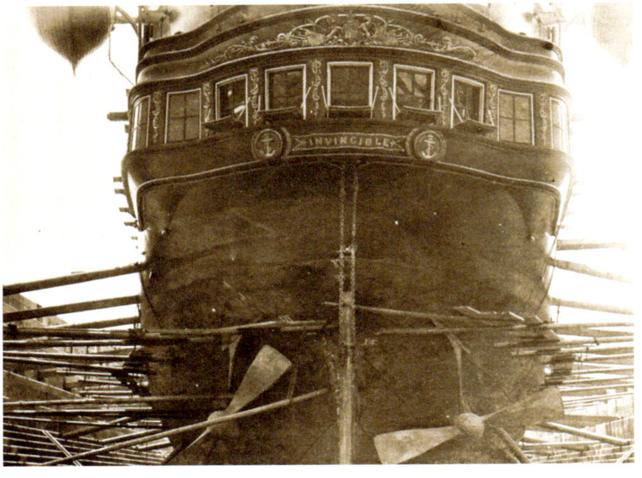

The first ship to enter No. 5 Dock was *Invincible*, seen here on that occasion. Through being the first ship to enter this dock, No. 5 Dock was from then on known as the 'Invincible Dock', a name which is now mostly forgotten but one that has an element of interest and would be worth returning it to.

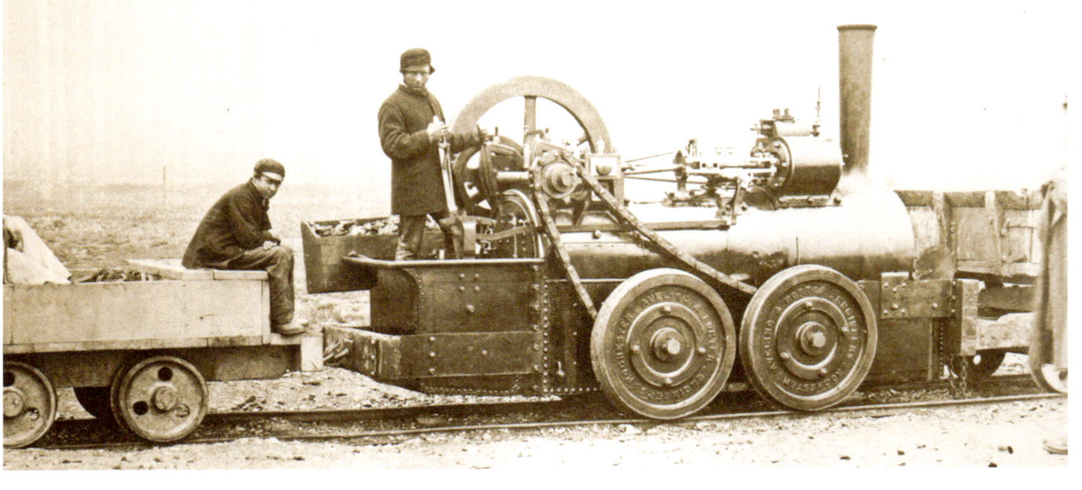

While convicts had initially been used to haul trucks by hand, steam engines manufactured by Aveling and Porter of Rochester were later acquired to undertake this work with greater efficiency.

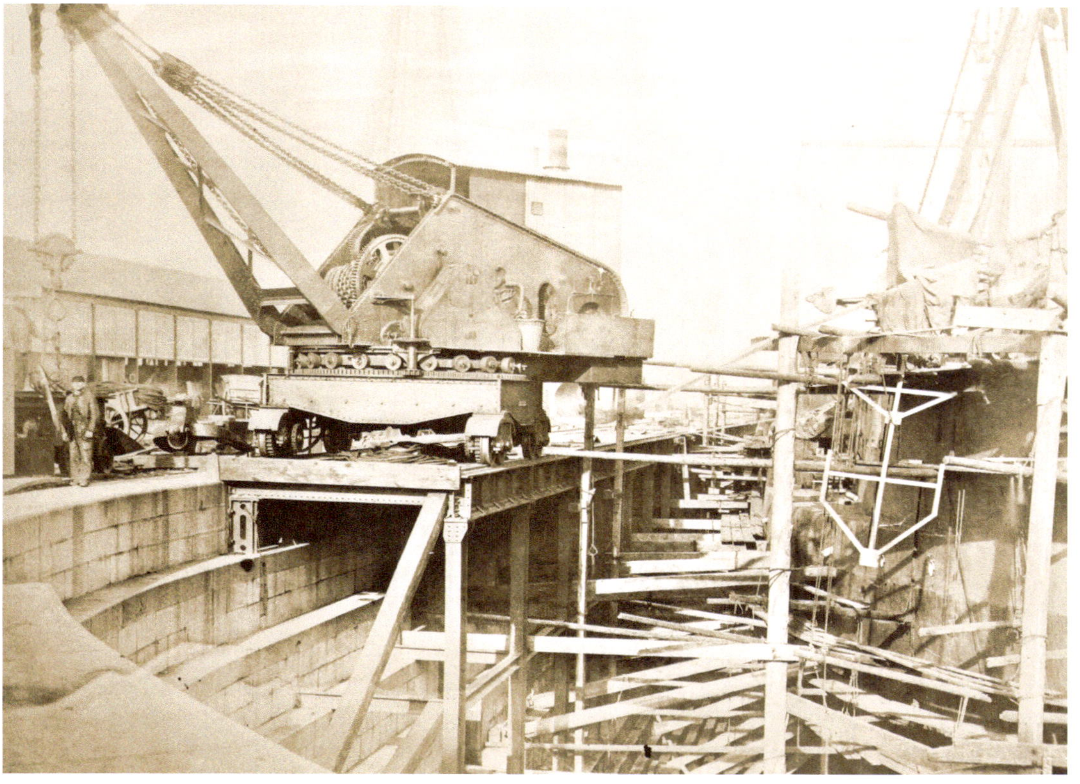

No. 6 Dock. Here the dock is viewed in February 1876, occupied by *Alexandria* (seen to the right of this photograph), a central battery ironclad that had been built at the Chatham end of the yard and launched from the No. 7 Slip in April of the previous year. The intention of this photograph was to show the method used for shoring a large warship when held in a dry dock.

For the hauling of heavy materials during the construction of the Gillingham extension to the yard, a tramway was built on site. One of the trucks for hauling material can be seen in the foreground of this photograph.

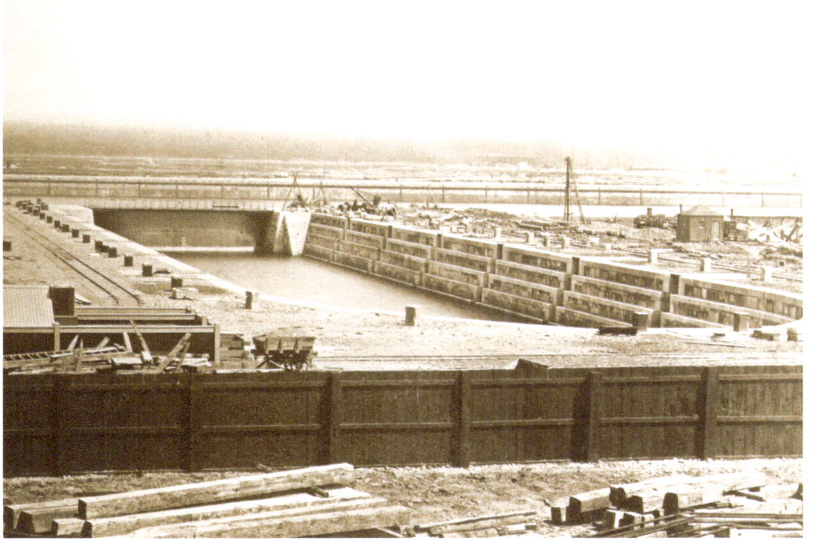

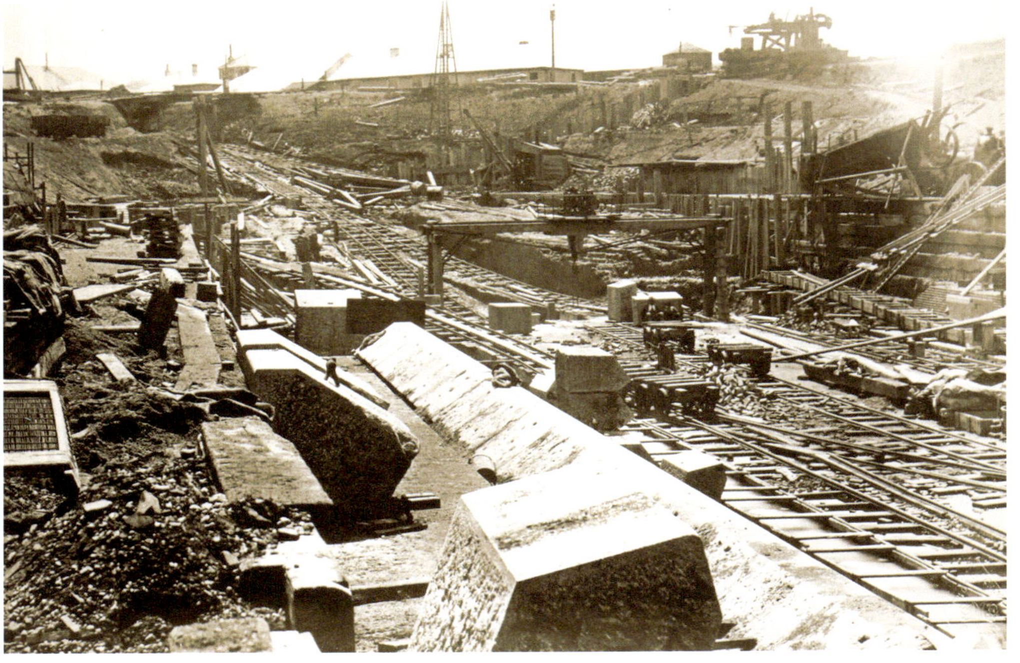

The extent and use of the tramway system within the dockyard can be readily appreciated from this photograph of work on the extension, a photograph taken in June 1872.

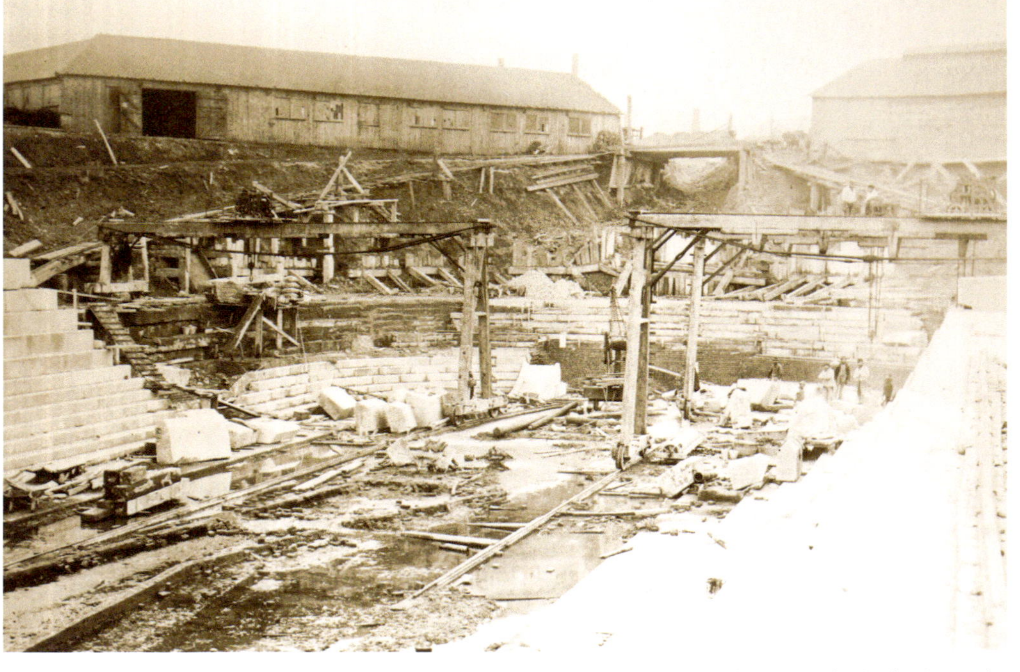

February 1872 and work is progressing nicely on No. 8 Dock, the last of the dry docks built on the south side of the Repairing Basin.

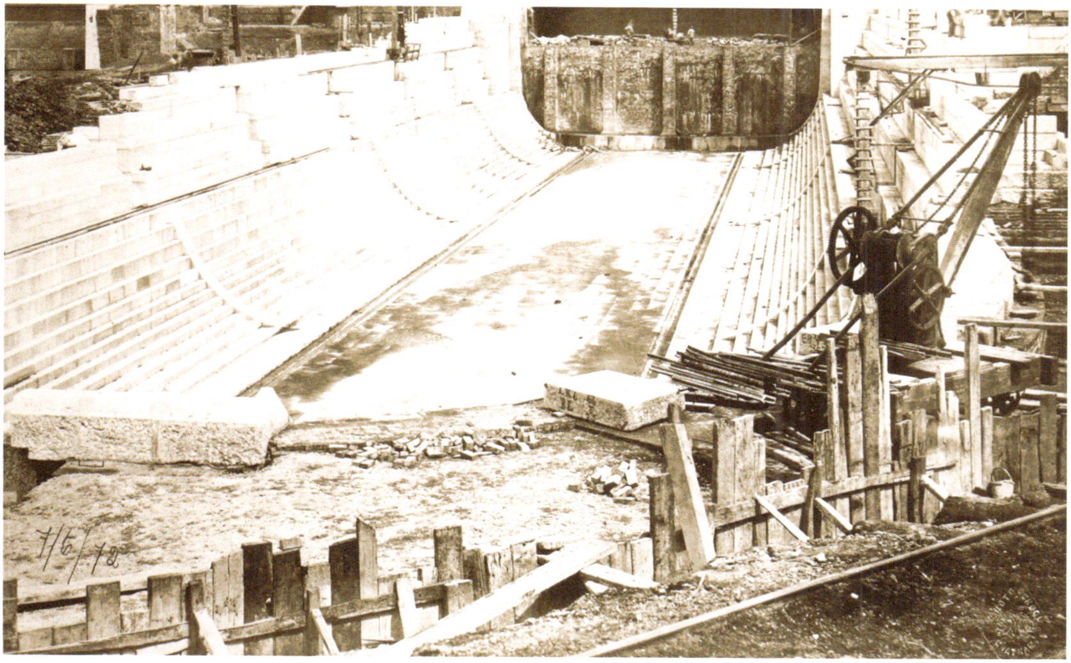

June 1872 and No. 8 Dock is nearing completion, but a further five months of work would still be required.

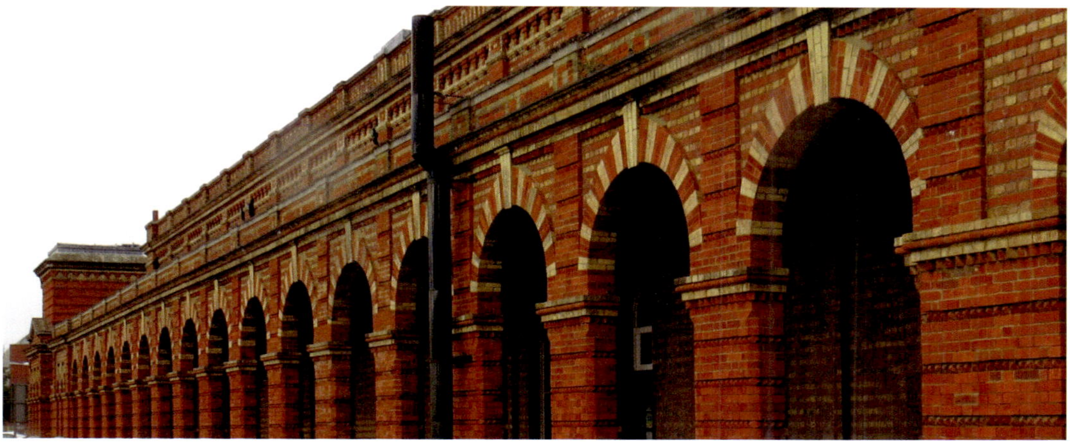

Essential to all the docks built around the Repairing Basin was the Dock Pumping Station that once held machinery supplied by Messrs J. and G. Rennie of Blackfriars for the pumping out of the four original docks that were annexed to the No. 1 Basin. The machinery was first trialled on 10 March 1874, running at 100 revolutions per minute. Within the building, a second, reserve engine was also in place, which at one time belonged to HMS *Forth*. On the occasion of the trial, 20,000 tons of water was pumped from one of the docks in 39 minutes, while the remaining 14,830 tons from the lower half was pumped in 66 minutes. The engine house itself, which has recently been restored, is a red-brick building, 77 feet in length, with an external arcade of brick piers. Immediately adjoining the engine house was the boiler house, which had the same external appearance and once housed nine separate boilers of the Cornish double flue style.

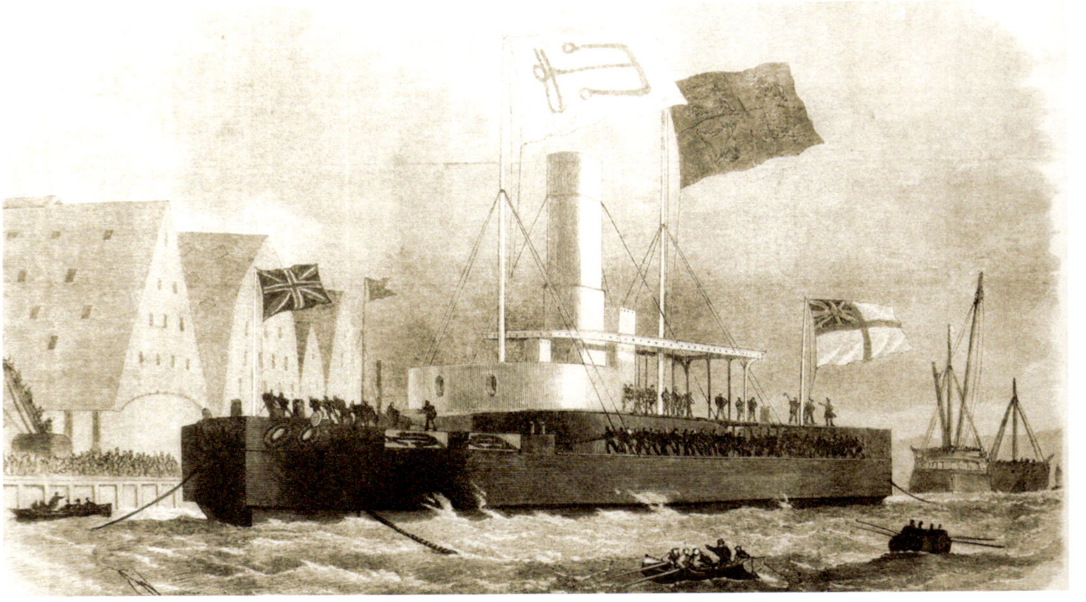

Here the ironclad monitor *Glatton* is seen on 8 March 1871, the day of her launch. It was constructed in the Chatham end of the yard (No. 3 Dock) and is being towed to the Gillingham end of the yard where she will enter the newly built Refitting Basin for completion.

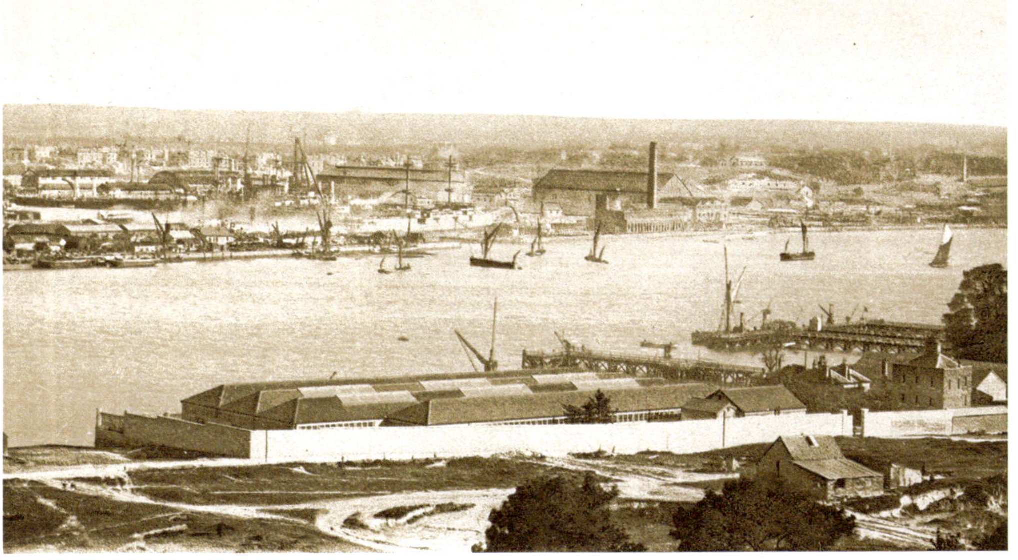

A turn of the century view across the Medway looking towards the extension. The Repairing Basin can be seen centre left, just beyond the River Medway. Once launched, or floated out, of dry dock, a vessel such as *Glatton* (see previous illustration) would be towed into the Repairing Basin for work to be undertaken on the upper deck. Surrounding each of the basins were various factory buildings, storehouses and workshops that were necessary to support the dedicated tasks undertaken on ships brought into each of these basins.

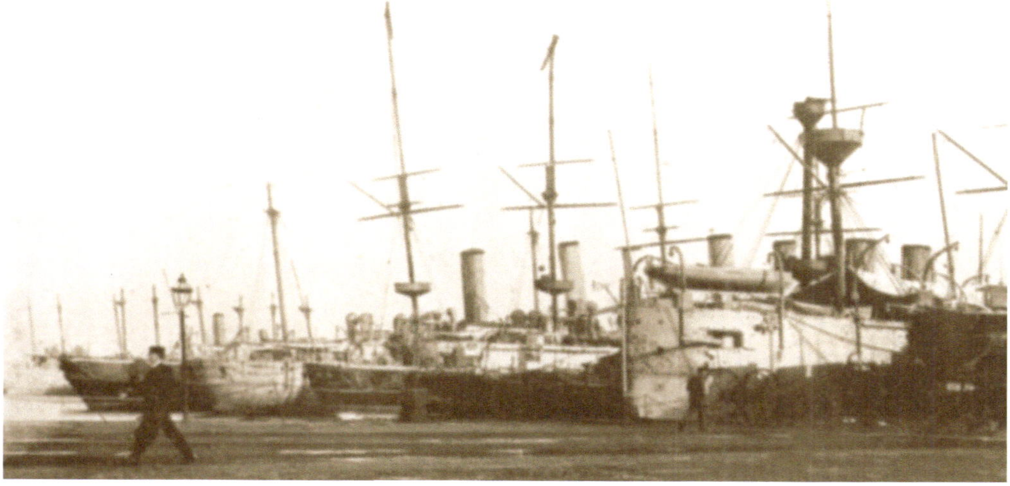

The Chatham Reserve Squadron, which consisted of older ships of the fleet, seen here *c.* 1906. During the summer, ships of the Reserve Squadron would leave the Gillingham end of the yard where they were based, touring popular seaside resorts to help create public enthusiasm for the Navy.

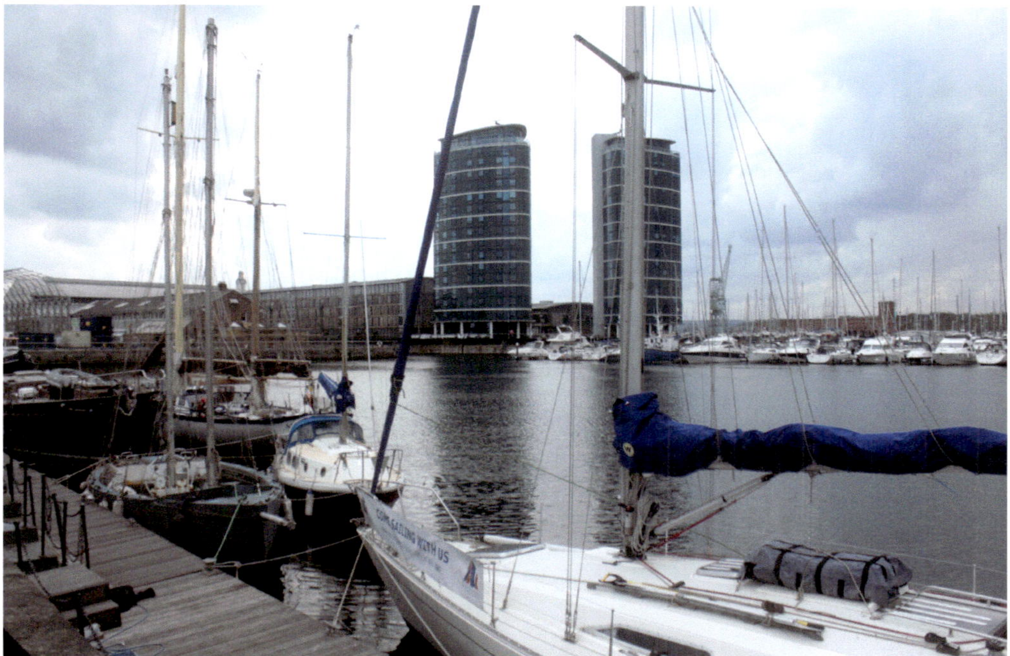

A modern-day view of the Repairing Basin and its immediate surrounds. Since closure of the dockyard this area of the former yard has seen considerable redevelopment, the emphasis being on residential and commercial accommodation.

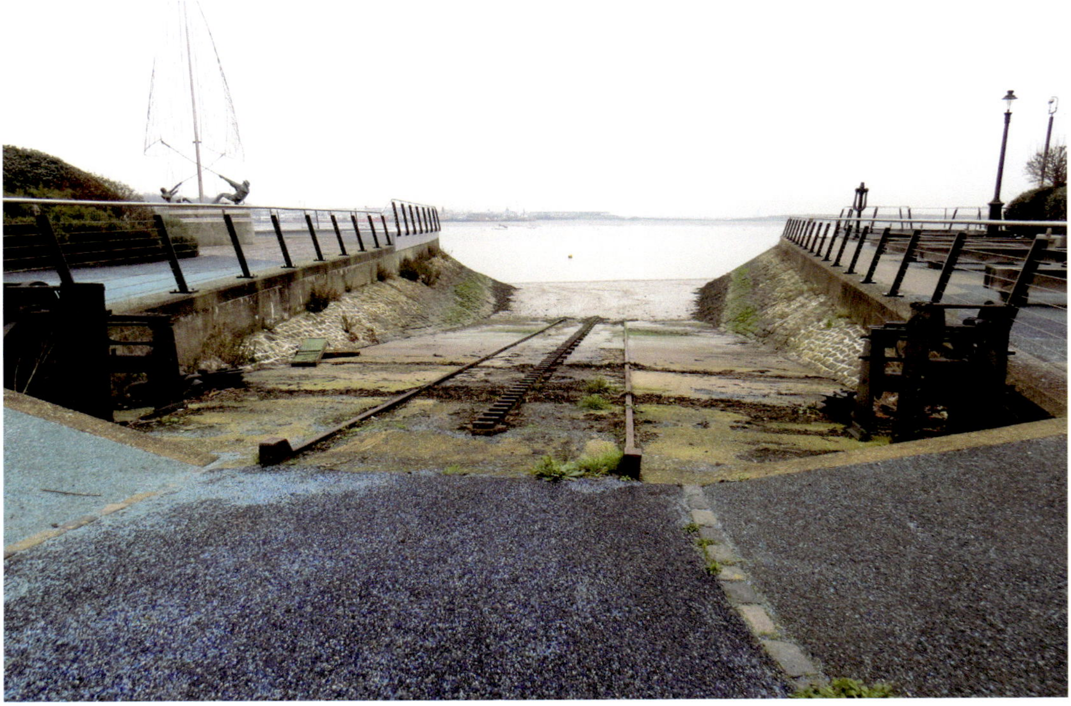

Among remaining features of the Gillingham extension, of which there are still a great many, is this unloading wharf located on the north side of St Mary's Island.

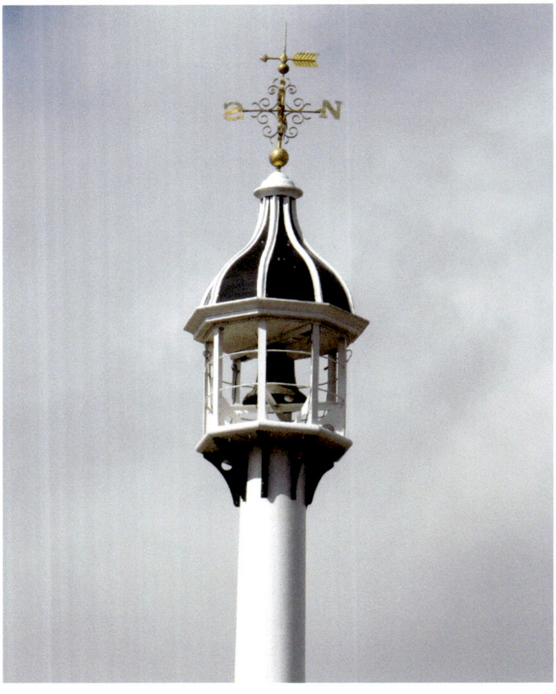

Another surviving feature of the Gillingham extension is this old dockyard bell standing close to the former Pembroke entrance gate. The bell would be rung shortly before the morning or afternoon start times to indicate that the dockyard gates would soon be closed and that those on their way into the yard needed to hurry. As the time grew closer to when the gates of the yard would close, the tolling of the bell became more rapid. If a worker had not passed through the gate by the time the bell had stopped tolling, a half-day's pay would be lost as entry into the yard would be refused until the next working session, either that same afternoon or the morning of the following day.

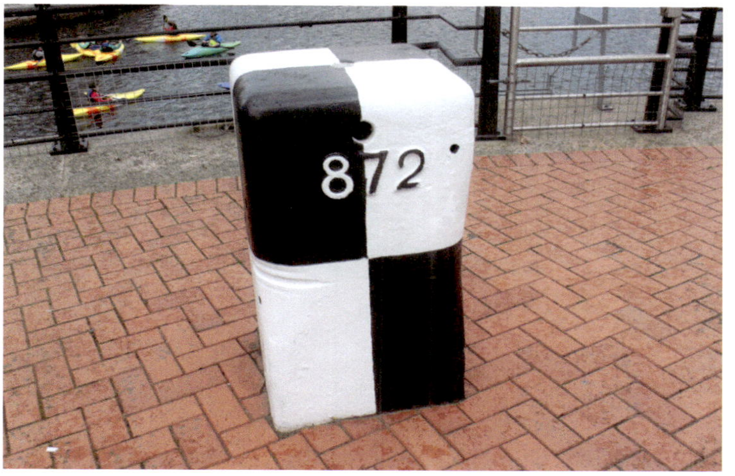

Around the basins and docks, bollards were placed for the tying up of ships while moored, each marked with the year in which that part of the extension was completed.

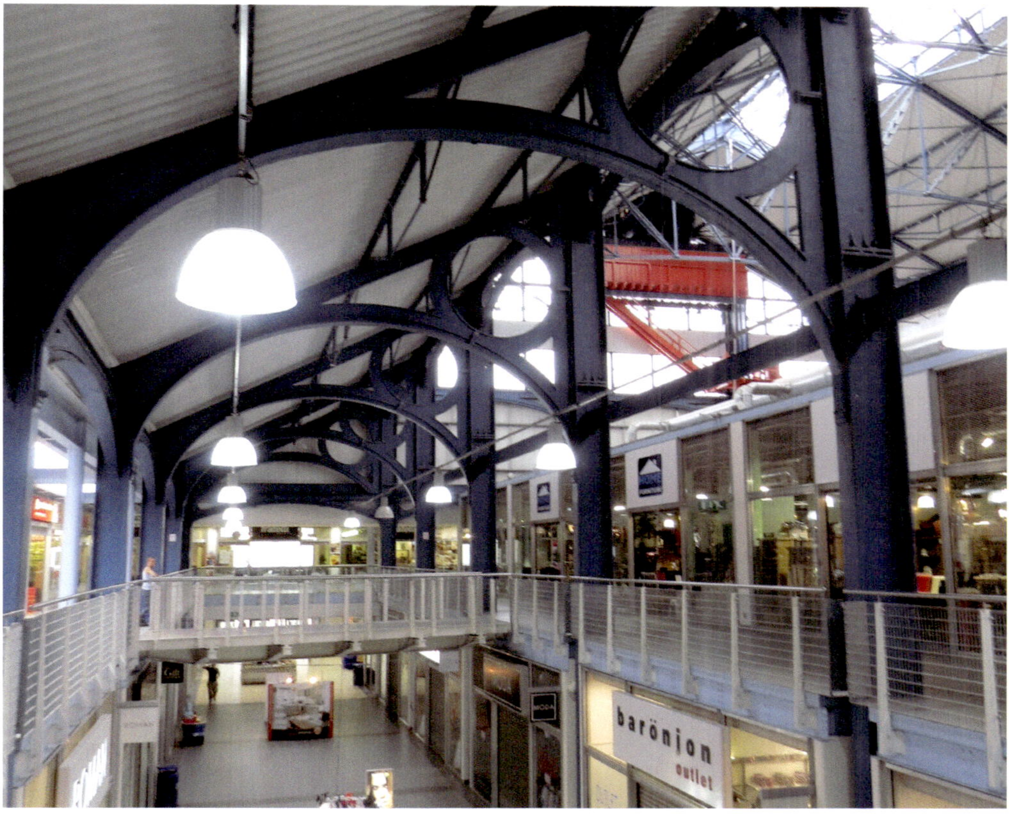

Dockside Outlet Centre is housed in the former Boiler Shop No. 1, a former Woolwich dockyard building slip. At the time of Woolwich dockyard closing in 1869, both this building and the framework of Machine Shop No. 8, which also still remains as a reminder of times past, were removed from the Woolwich yard and re-erected on the spot where both now stand. The cost of this removal and re-erection programme was estimated to be £6,000, considerably less than the outlay that would have been required for the construction of two completely new buildings.

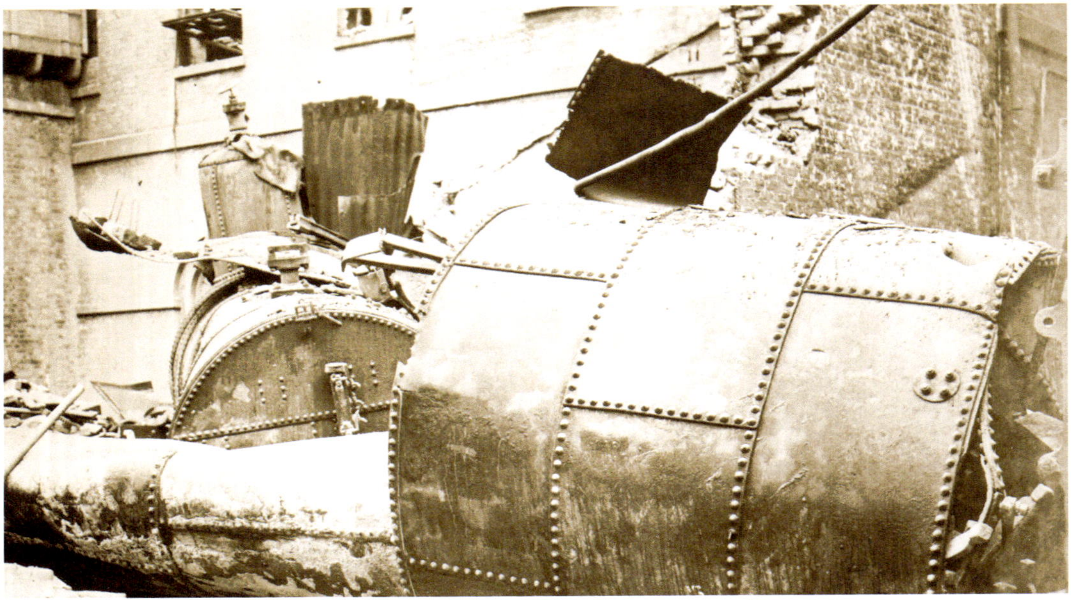

Danger lurked in the dockyard for those who worked there. One particular incident occurred in September 1866 when two workmen were killed when a boiler exploded in the hammer house. According to an inquest held on the two men, the cause of the explosion was regarded as an accident, the boiler at the time having an 'insufficiency' of water.

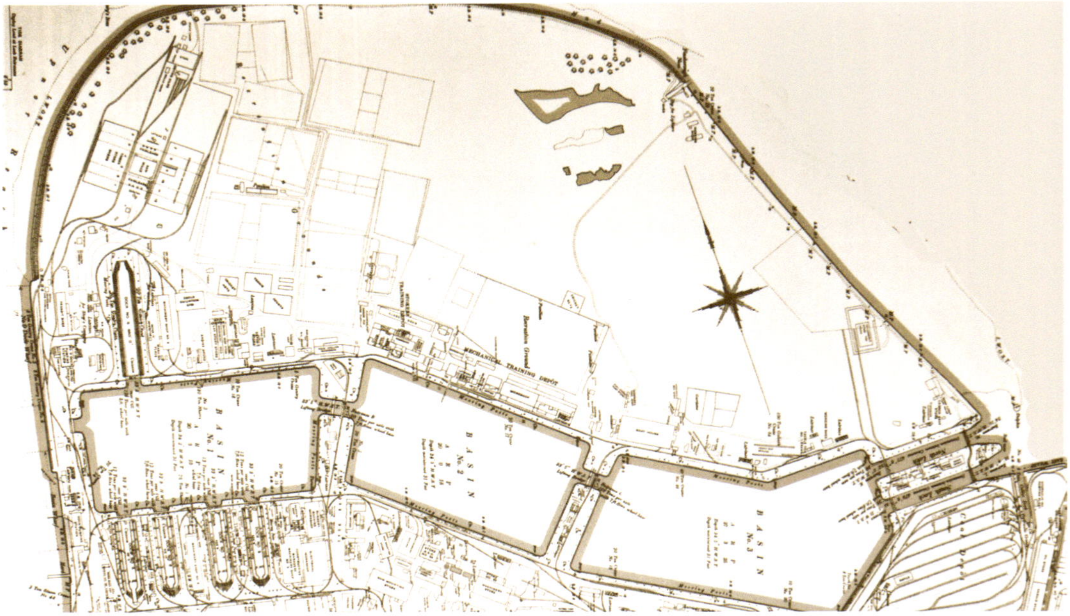

By 1943 and the date of this plan of the dockyard, much of the area of St Mary's Island, which had been taken by the Admiralty for future expansion, had now seen construction of a variety of new buildings to facilitate the repair, refitting and building of naval warships and other craft.

5

The Naval Connection

While strictly speaking the Royal Dockyard that came to St Mary's Island is naval and provides a naval connection to Gillingham, this is only in the sense of constructing and repairing warships. The dockyard was a civilian branch of the Navy and, as such, those employed within its gates were administered separately from those who served within the ranks of the Royal Navy and went to sea. The seagoing side of the Navy also came to be well represented in Gillingham, for the men who served required living accommodation, medical facilities and entertainment.

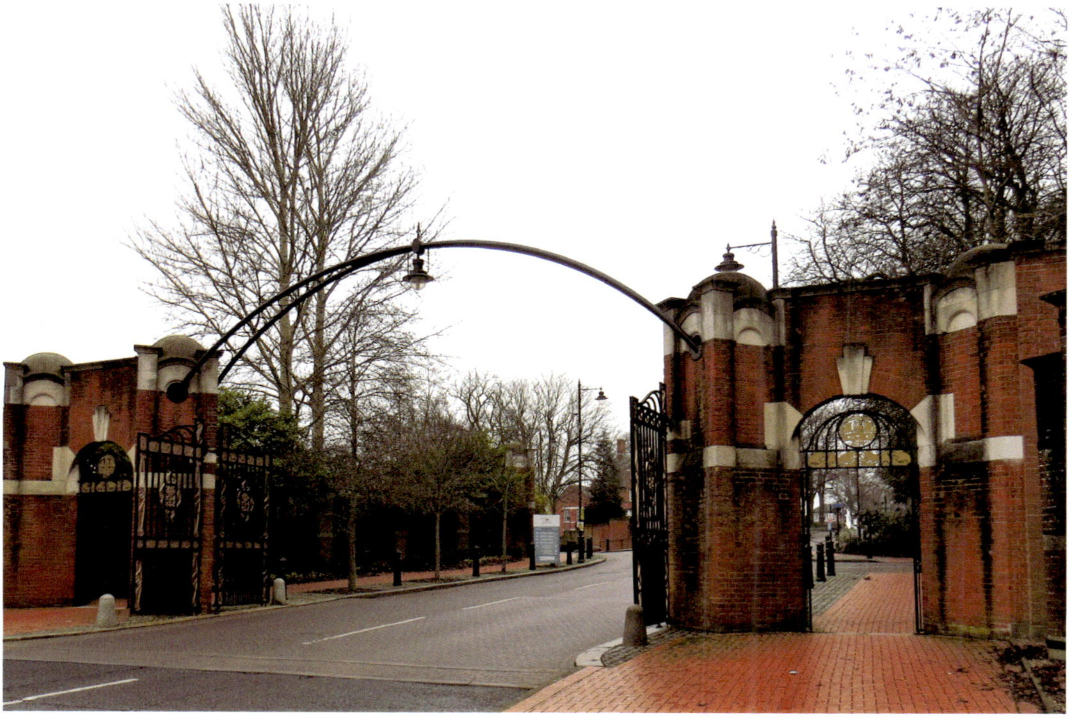

HMS Pembroke, the name given to the Chatham Royal Naval Barracks, was first occupied in December 1902 and, following the withdrawal of the Royal Navy from Gillingham, closed on 31 March 1984. The gate, as seen here, together with most of the original buildings, still remain, now used to house the Medway campus of two major universities.

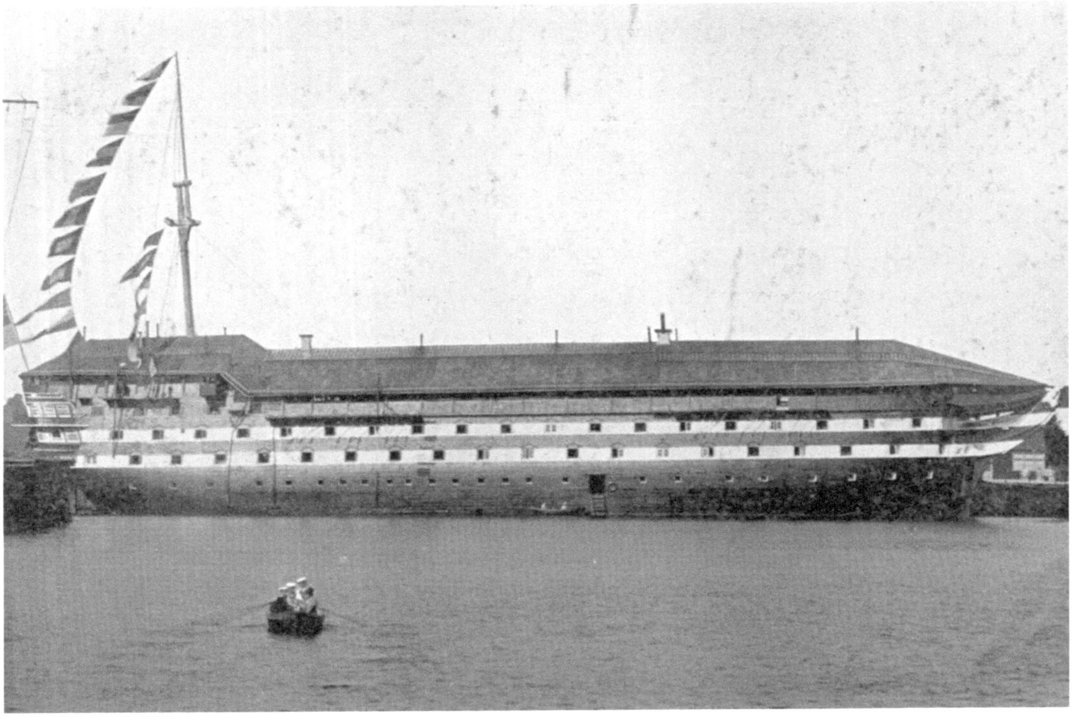

Prior to the construction of the barracks, seamen of the Royal Navy belonging to Chatham were housed in hulks moored in the Medway, with the original depot ship, *Pembroke*, seen here, which bestowed her name upon the barracks.

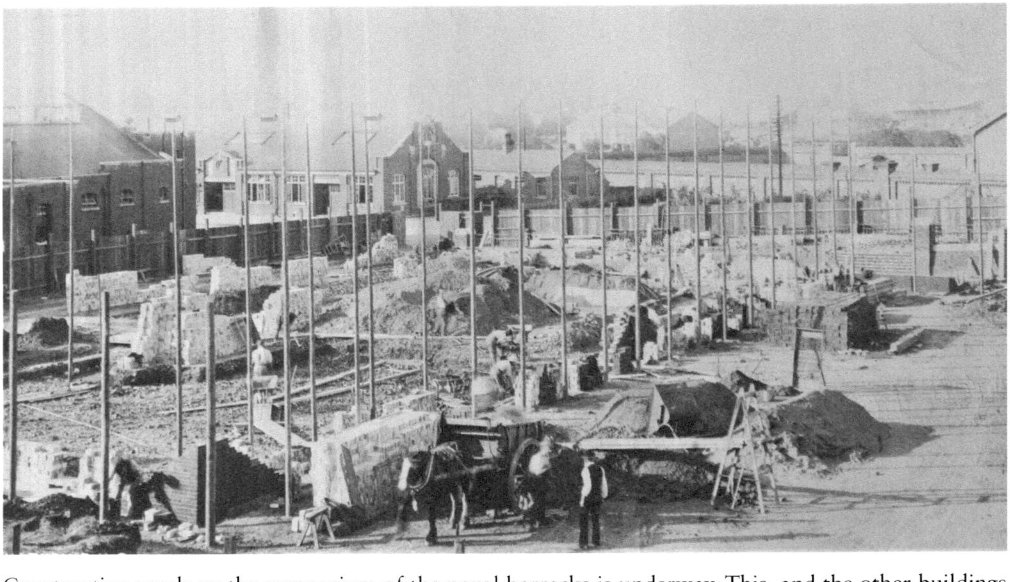

Construction work on the gymnasium of the naval barracks is underway. This, and the other buildings that made up the barracks, were built under the supervision of the Naval Works Department, with Holloway Brothers of London undertaking the work. The designer was Sir Henry Pilkington.

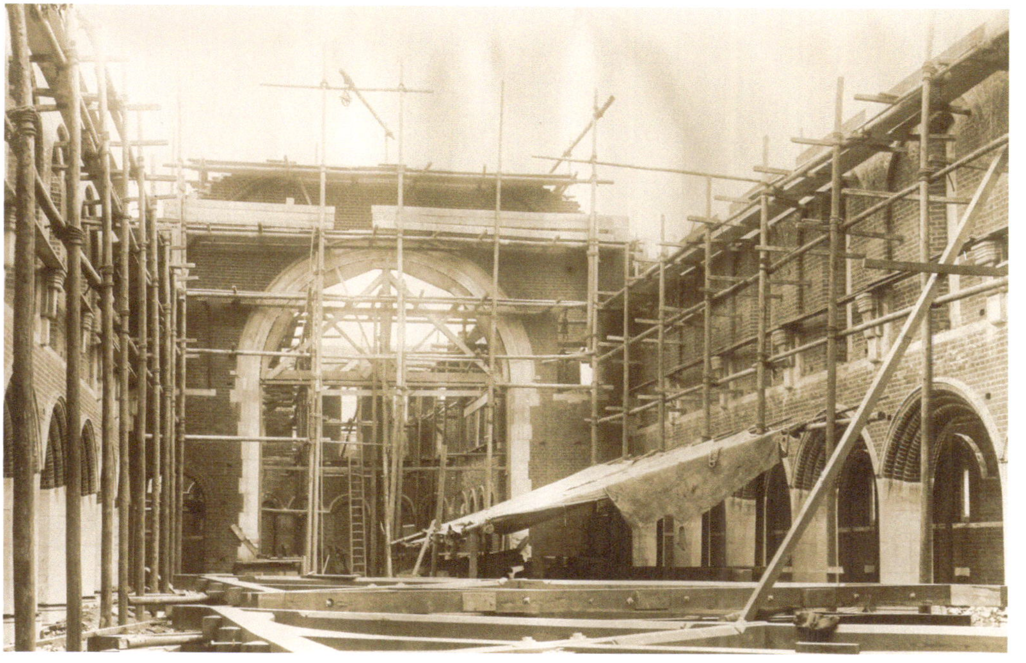

Building work continued long after the accommodation blocks were put in use. One of the later buildings was St George's Chapel, seen here under construction on 31 August 1905. The foundation stone of the chapel had been laid on 27 April 1905, and on completion the building was dedicated by the Bishop of Rochester, John Harmer, on 19 December 1906.

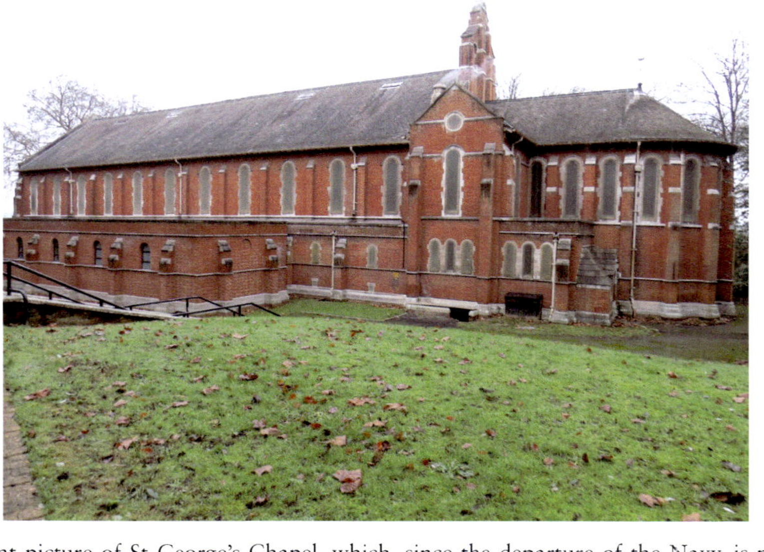

A more recent picture of St George's Chapel, which, since the departure of the Navy, is managed by Medway Council. Within the chapel there are many naval memorials including a stained-glass window unveiled on 29 October 1950 by Princess Elizabeth (the future Queen Elizabeth) to commemorate Chatham-based ships that were lost during the Second World War.

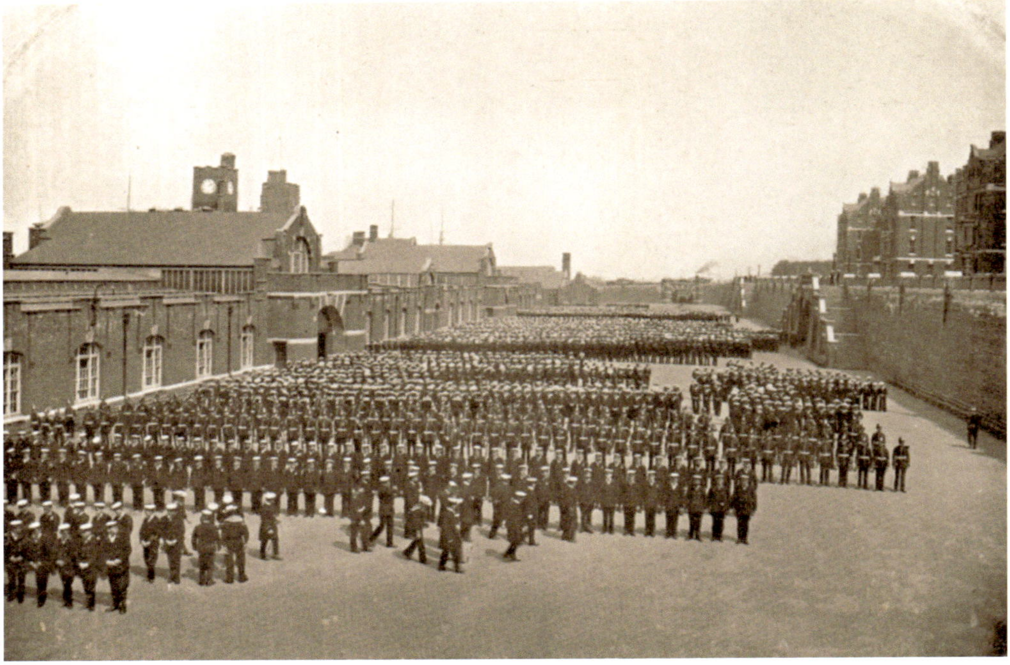

The seamen attached to Pembroke Barracks are seen here on parade during 1903, the time of its first inspection, which was undertaken by Admiral A. H. Markham, Commander-in-Chief at the Nore.

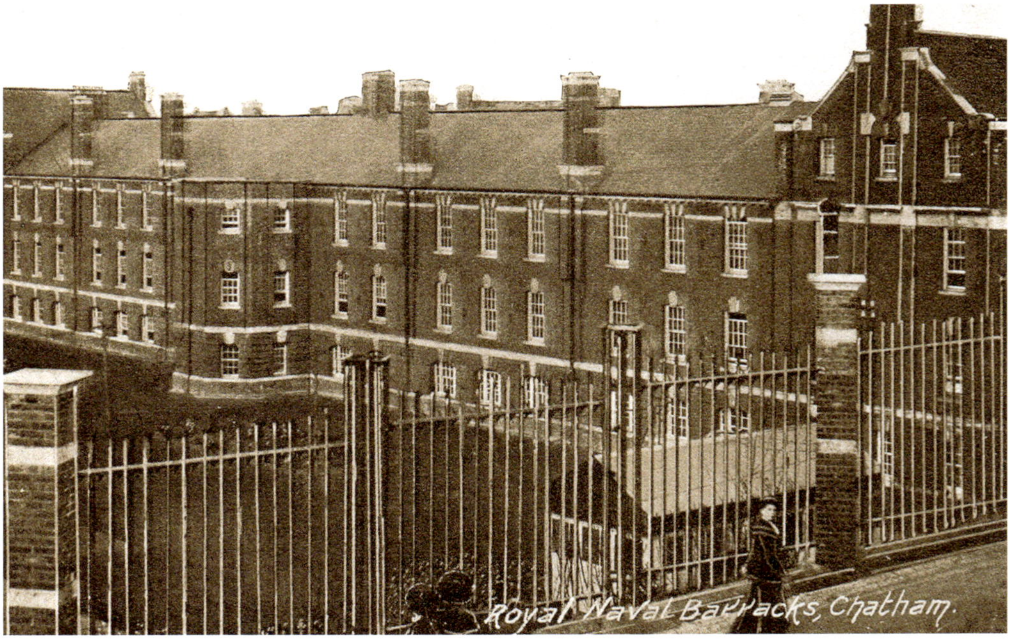

A general view of Pembroke's accommodation blocks shortly after their construction. Building work on HMS Pembroke began in May 1897, with the barracks first occupied in December 1902. By May of the following year, the barracks housed some 4,600 naval personnel.

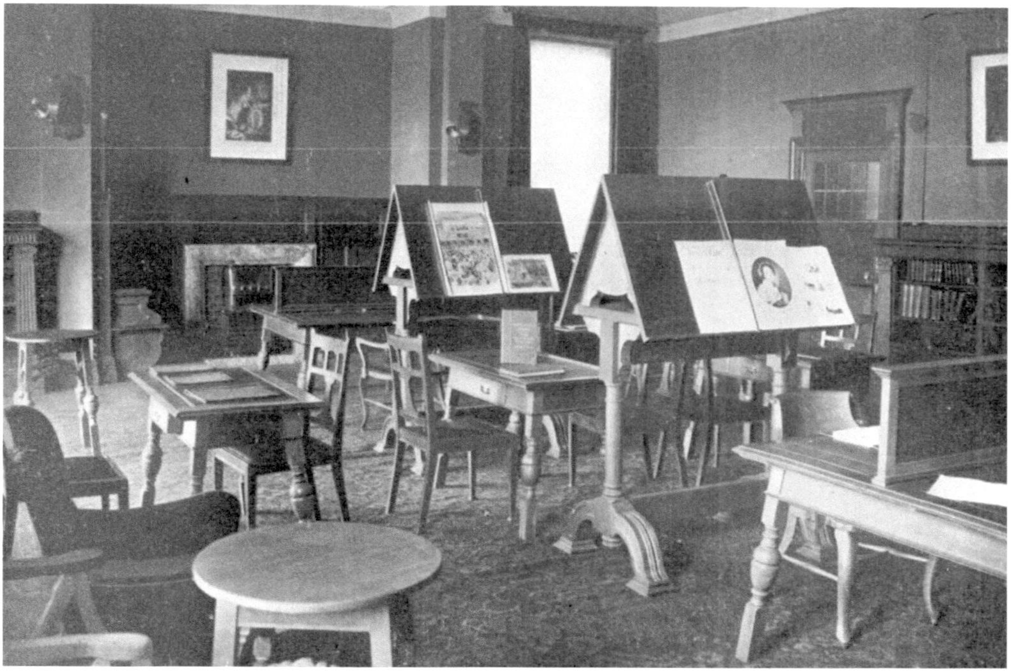
The standard and nature of accommodation differed according to rank. This is the Officers' Library.

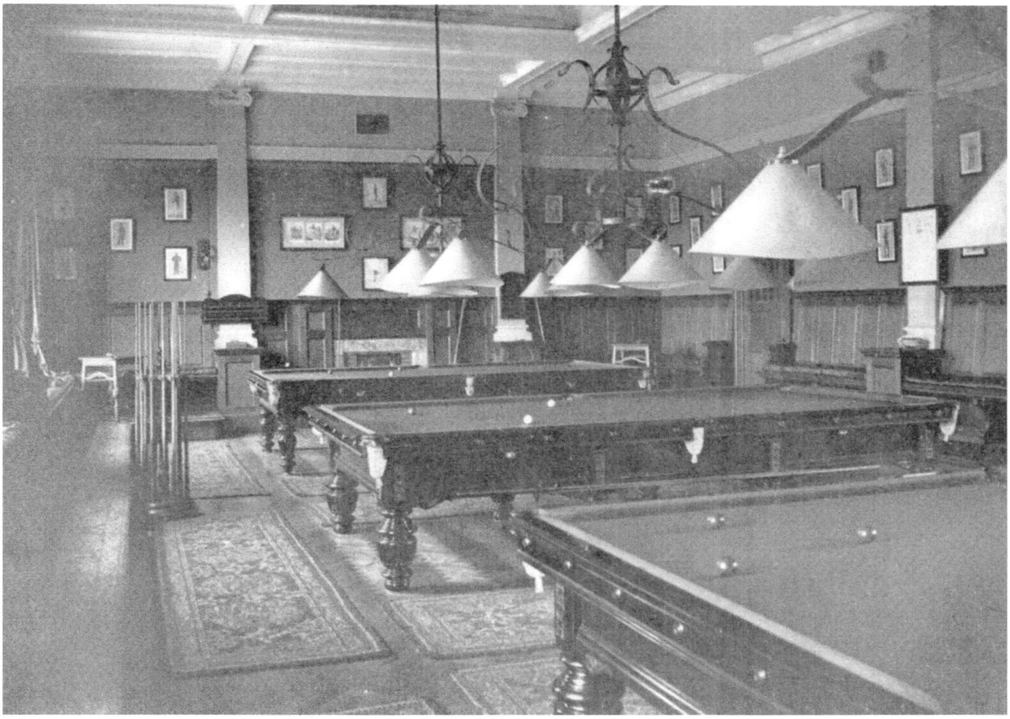
The Officers' Billiard Room had a similar club room luxury that was denied to the other ranks.

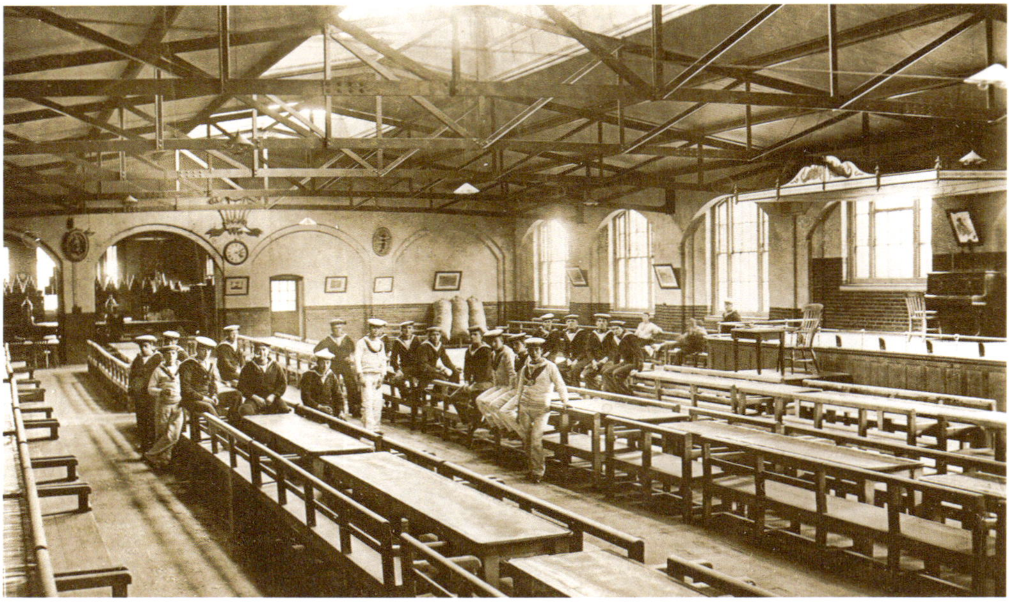

The canteen used by the ratings – an altogether more basic facility.

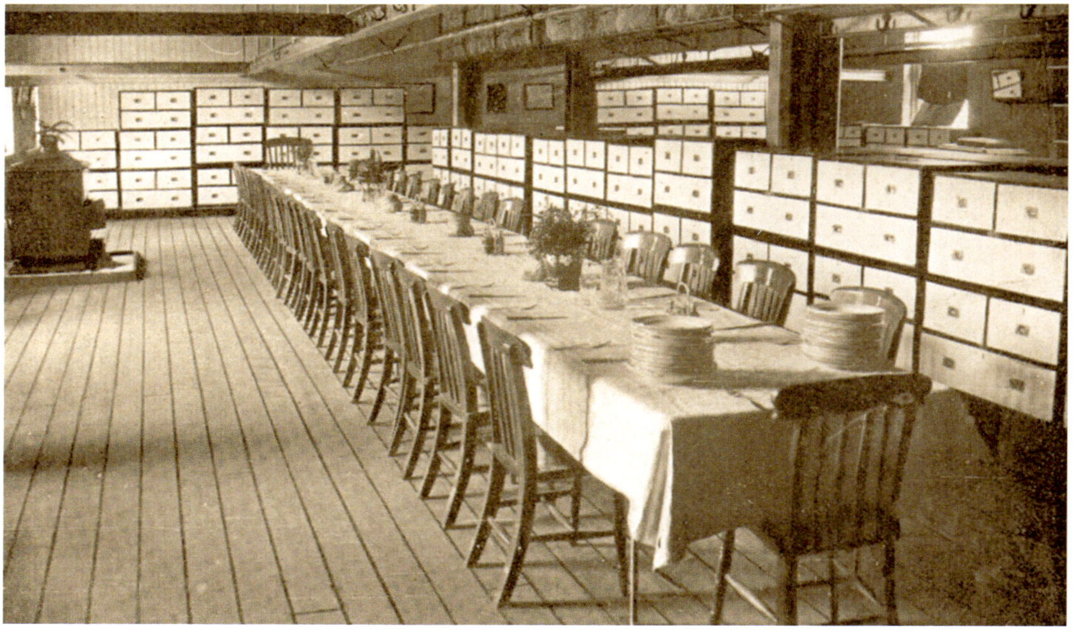

The Chief Stokers' Mess.

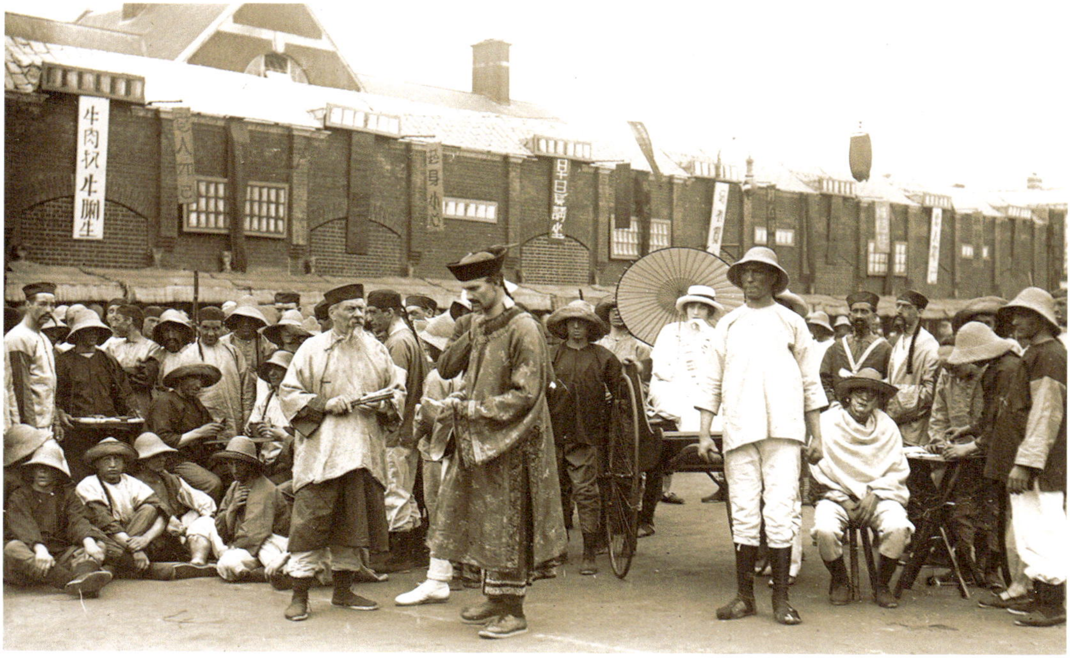

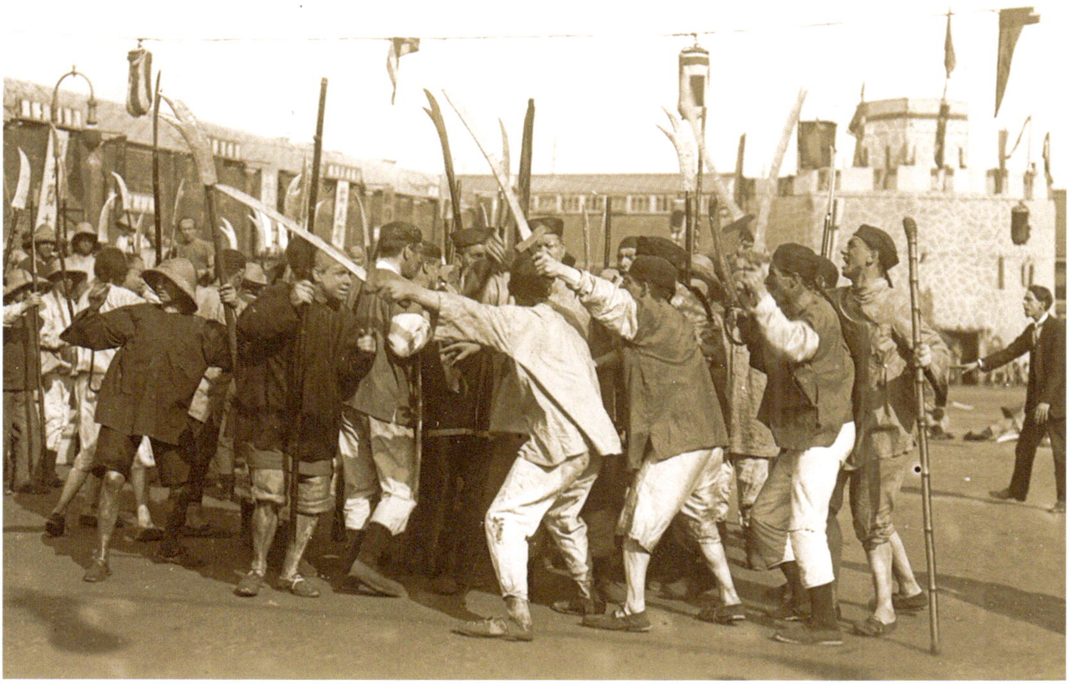

To enthuse the local populace into naval affairs and support the Navy across the Empire, the Royal Naval Barracks held open days with shows to excite public interest. The open day held in September 1913 saw a re-enactment of the Navy's role in the Boxer Rebellion of 1900.

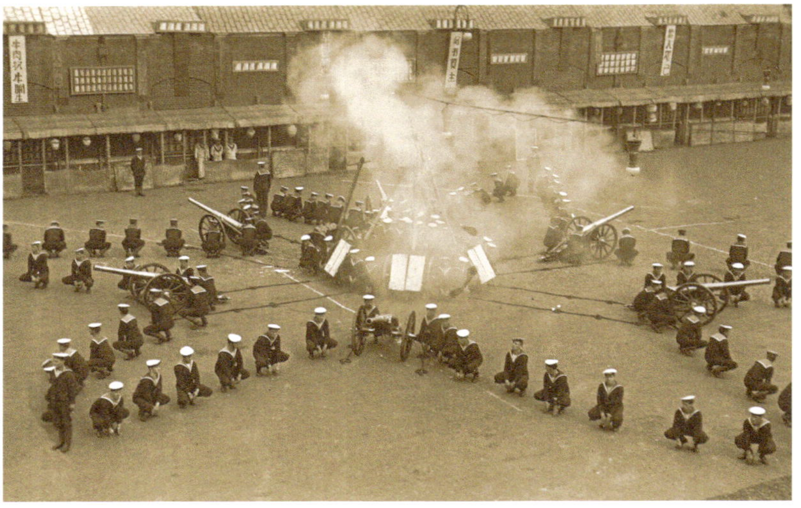

Open days also saw gunnery displays in which teams competed to assemble and fire field guns.

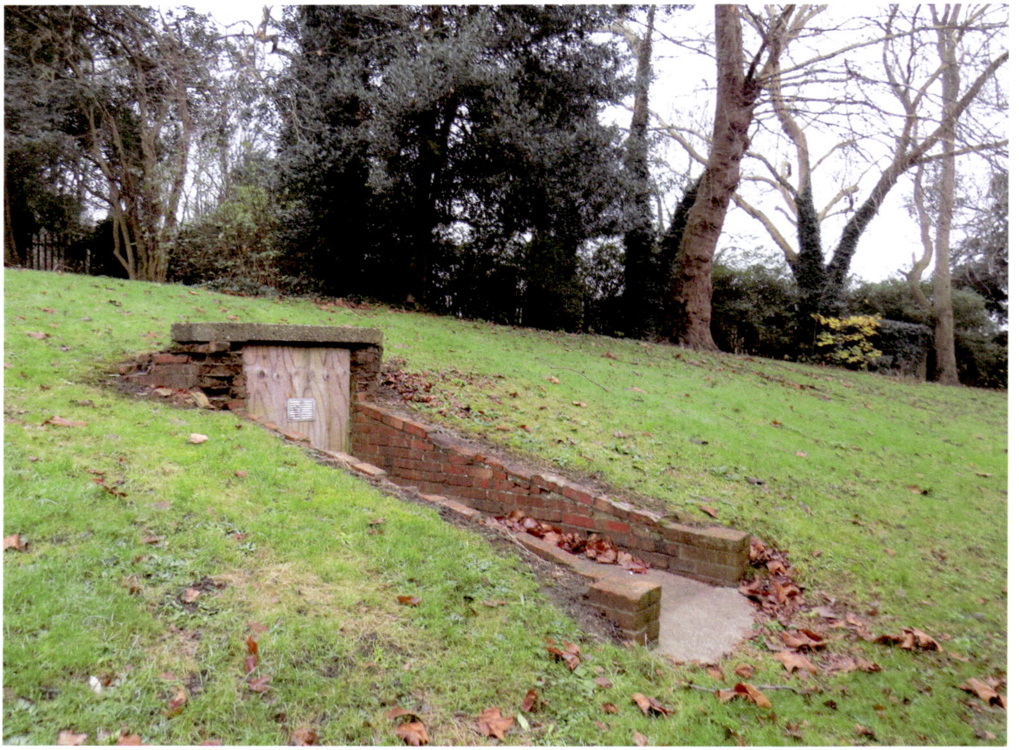

In preparation for the outbreak of the Second World War air-raid shelters, of which this is the entrance to one of them, were built within the area of the barracks. This was a sound policy given that the naval barracks during the First World War had suffered one of the most devastating raids of the entire war. On 3 September 1917 a German Gotha bomber dropped a 110-pound bomb onto the naval barracks, causing the death of 136 ratings. Helping ensure such a considerable loss of life was that the bomb hit the drill hall, which at the time provided additional sleeping quarters. Unfortunately, the drill hall had been built with a glass roof, resulting in thousands of flying shards of glass that added to the number of victims.

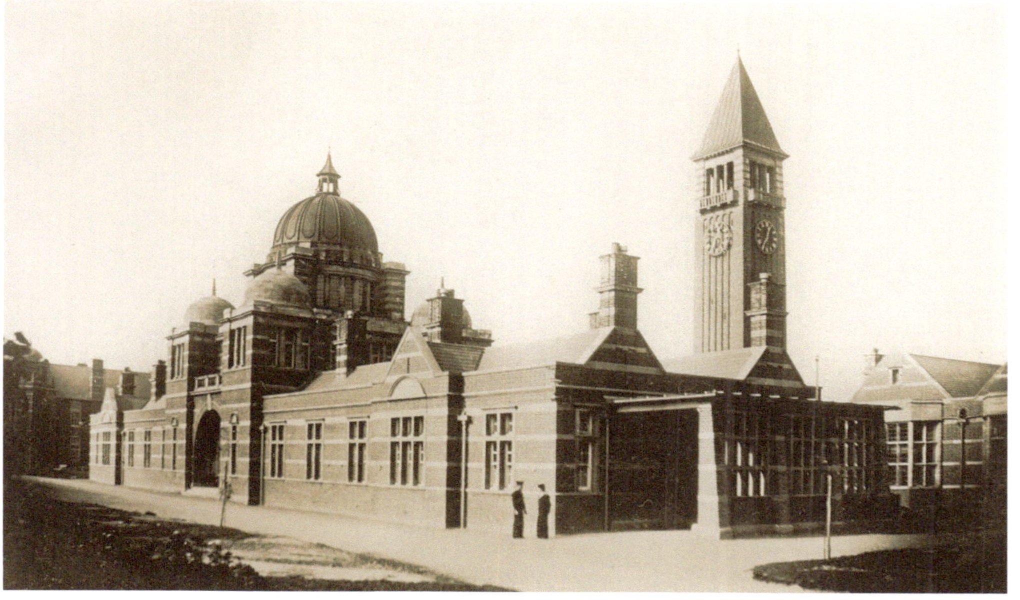

Medway Maritime Hospital, Windmill Road. Originally built for the Royal Navy and opened in 1905, it replaced an earlier naval hospital, Melville Hospital, built in Chatham. The new hospital was three times the size of the old Melville Hospital, constructed on a 29-acre site that gave plenty of room for expansion. Designed by J. T. C. Murray, the building was given a distinctive facing of red brick and Doulton stone quarried in Somerset. For those with contagious diseases there was a separate zymotic hospital on the same site.

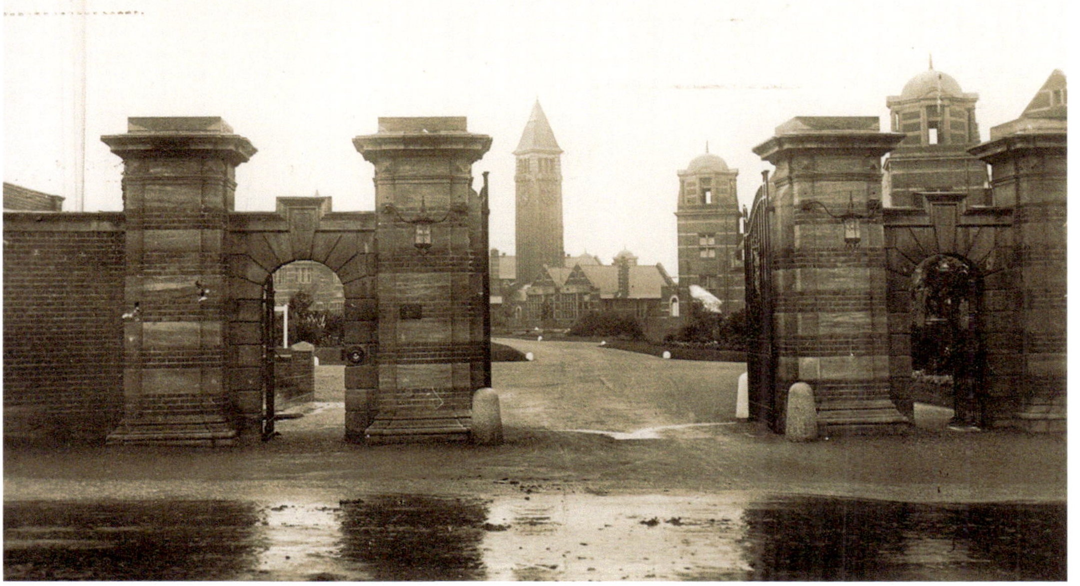

The original entryway into the naval hospital as seen shortly after the hospital's opening in 1905.

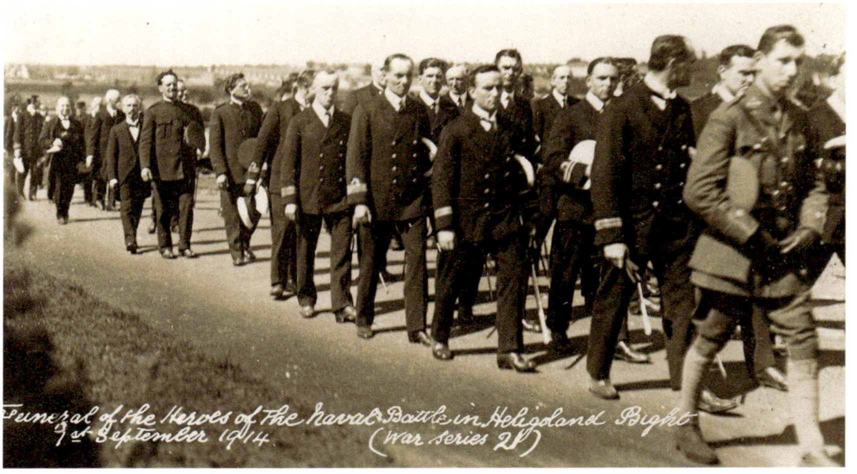

The Royal Naval Barracks being within the boundary of Gillingham meant that naval funerals were often held at the parish church, 'St Mary's on the Green'. Many lives were lost during the First World War, and the first major set of casualties to be brought to the church were those who died during an action fought on 28 August 1914 in the south-eastern North Sea off Heligoland Bight. In total thirty-five British seamen were killed in this, the first Anglo-German naval battle of that war.

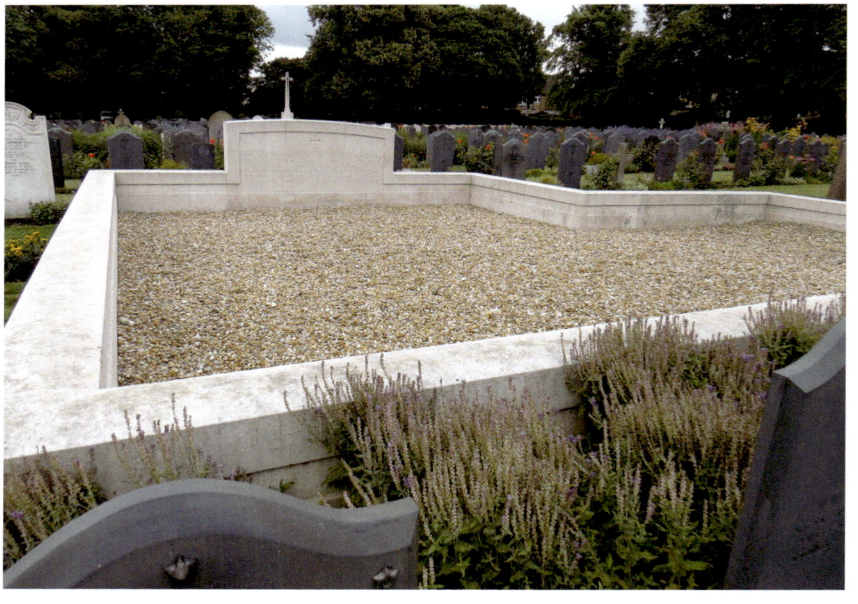

A far greater loss of life took place in November 1914 when the battleship *Bulwark* blew up in the Medway while moored in Kethole Reach. The fear at the time was that the explosion was the result of a torpedo fired by a German submarine, but ultimately the cause was considered most likely an accident, the ship being badly designed and prone to an internal explosion that once set off in one part of the ship, possibly by a member of the crew illicitly smoking, would cascade throughout the ship. Over seventy lives were lost, with their remains placed in this memorial grave within the cemetery of St Mary's Church, alongside those who died when another naval ship, *Princess Irene*, an auxiliary minelayer, also blew up in the Medway during the following year.

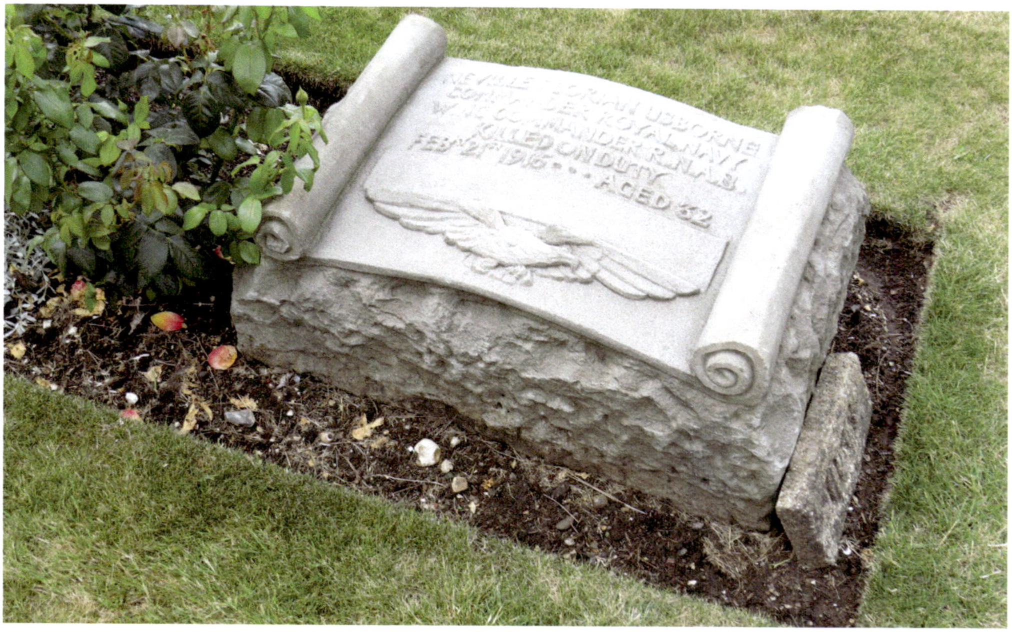

Another naval officer, killed in February 1916, buried in the cemetery at Gillingham is Commander Neville Usborne, an aviation pioneer and at the time the commanding officer of the naval airship station at nearby Kingsnorth. He died alongside Squadron Commander de Courcy Ireland while trying out a new experimental device, known as an airship-plane, designed to meet the increasing number of Zeppelins conducting bombing raids on British cities. The device consisted of an airship envelope attached to a fully working BE2c aeroplane, with the aeroplane lifted into the air by the hydrogen-filled envelope, then unhooked when a Zeppelin was reported. Unfortunately, one of three hooks holding the aeroplane failed to disconnect, with the aeroplane becoming entangled in the descending envelope, crashing to the ground and killing its two occupants.

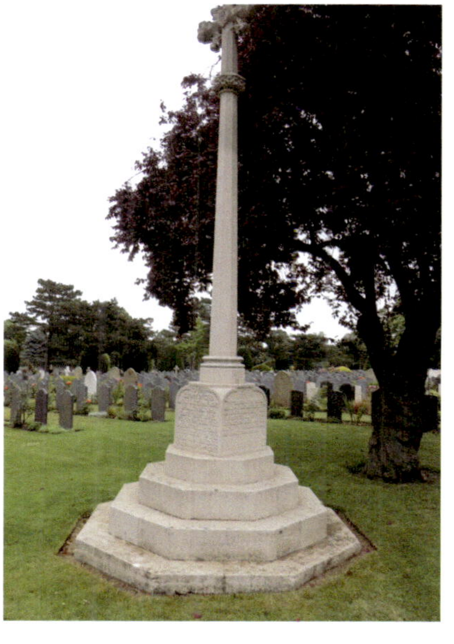

The memorial in the churchyard to those who died in the air raid on the naval barracks on 3 September 1917, which took the lives of 136 naval ratings.

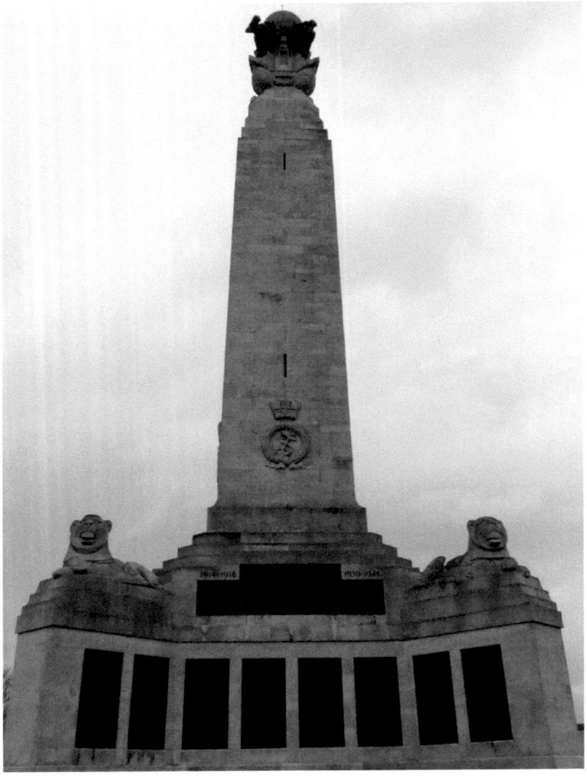

Naval war memorial. As a one-time principal manning port for the Royal Navy, this memorial, alongside similar ones at Portsmouth and Plymouth, was dedicated, following the ending of the First World War, to the sailors, airmen and marines of the Royal Navy who lost their lives but had no known grave. Designed by Sir Robert Lorimer, the one here, which overlooks Chatham but is located just inside the borders of Gillingham, originally contained 8,515 names. Upon the ending of the Second World War, each of the three memorials, including the one overlooking Chatham, was expanded and given a surround that includes an additional 10,098 names.

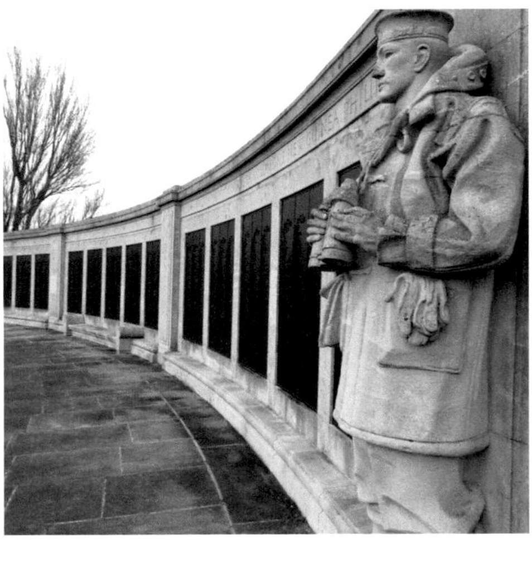

Detail of the surround, which, like the original obelisk, is of Portland stone. This is one of four statues of sailors. The surround was unveiled by the Duke of Edinburgh on 15 October 1952 and is maintained by the Commonwealth War Graves Commission.

6

Everyday Life

With the dockyard extension creating a huge industrial monolith within Gillingham that would employ over 10,000 by the end of the First World War, the town that developed and supported that workforce had to meet every imaginable need. Homes for the workforce quickly spiralled outwards from Gillingham Gate, the number of shops and pubs soon multiplied by the dozen and a number of new churches, chapels and cinemas were soon added. Not far behind was the emergence of a sophisticated transport system (initially trams but later buses) that allowed even the most rural and outstretched parts of the parish to be engulfed by housing estates.

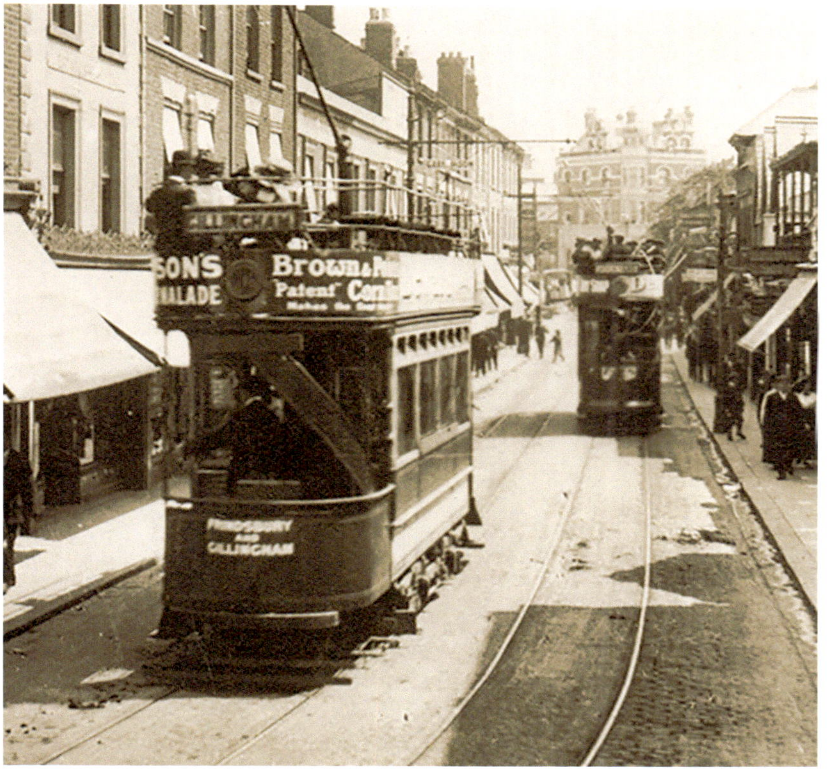

A general view of the High Street seen here *c.* 1905. A tramway through Medway had begun operating in June 1902, with trams connecting Borstal, Frindsbury, Strood, Rochester and Chatham to Old Brompton and Gillingham town centre, with those running into and terminating at either Gillingham Green or Victoria Bridge. In addition, a service also ran into Gillingham by way of Chatham Hill and Watling Street, with that service later extended into Rainham.

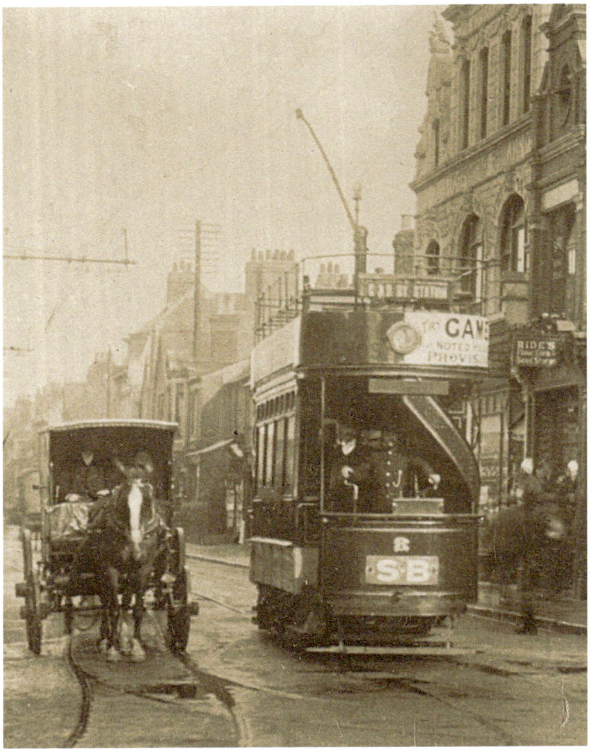

This tram, seen here in the High Street, is serving route SB, a route that takes in Chatham railway station via Old Brompton and Chatham Town Hall.

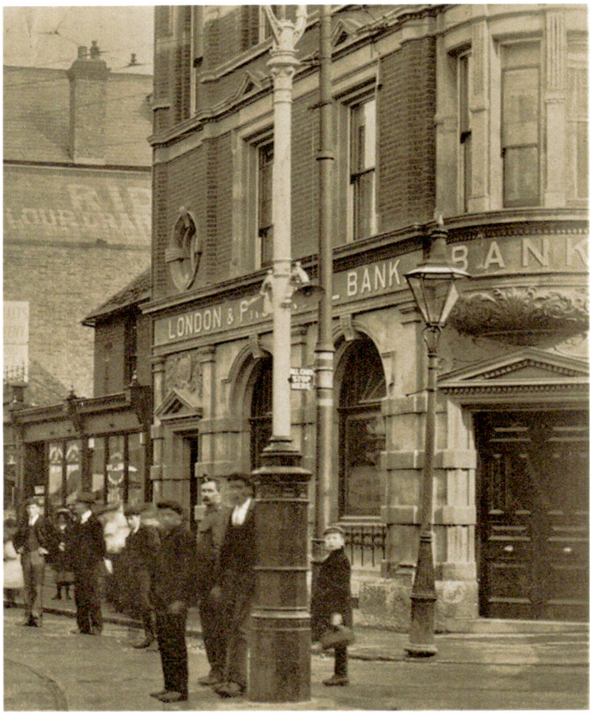

Queueing for a tram at the tram stop position on the corner of the High Street and Canterbury Street, just outside the London and Provincial Bank (No. 77 High Street).

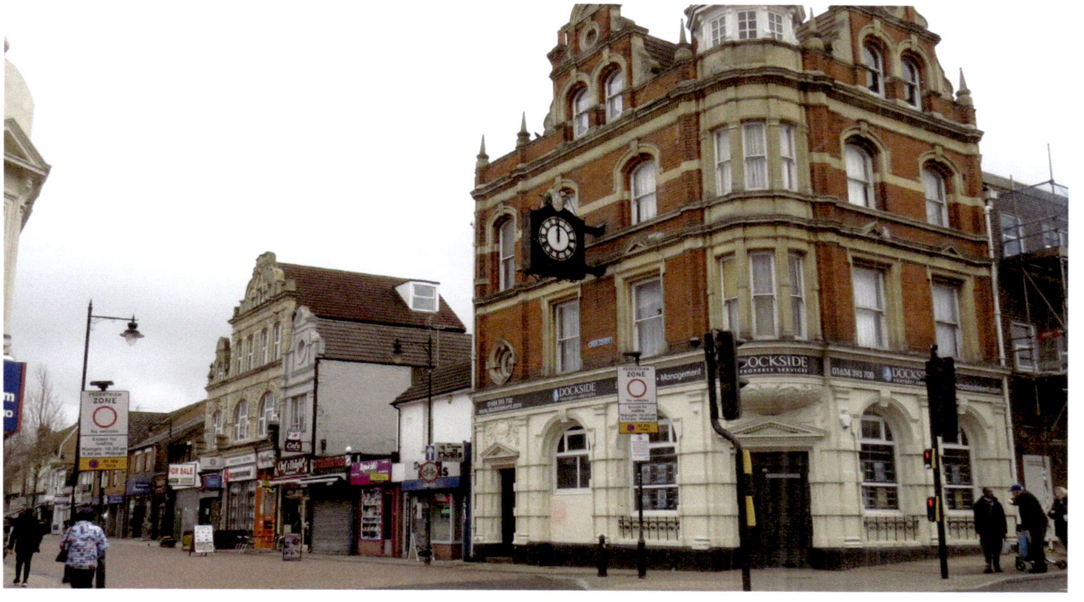

Above: By 1918 the London and Provincial Bank (see illustration on previous page) had been subsumed into Barclays Bank, but more recently it changed hands as can be seen in this modern-day photograph.

Below right: Bank Chambers (No. 84 High Street) has housed a number of different shops and enterprises over the years, but is pictured here because of its impressive design, one often unnoticed by those more intent on shopping. For several decades, going back to at least the 1920s, it was the premises of E. A. Stewart Wine & Spirits merchant, but the building at different times has also housed a dentist, an opticians, the local office of the Woolwich Building Society and, as seen in this picture, a shoe repair shop and jewellers.

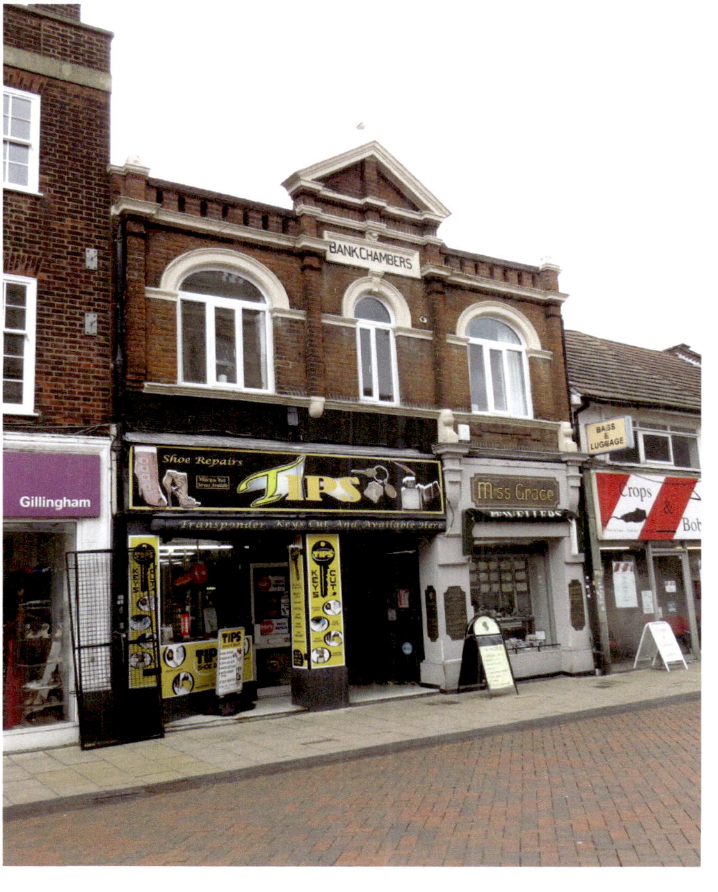

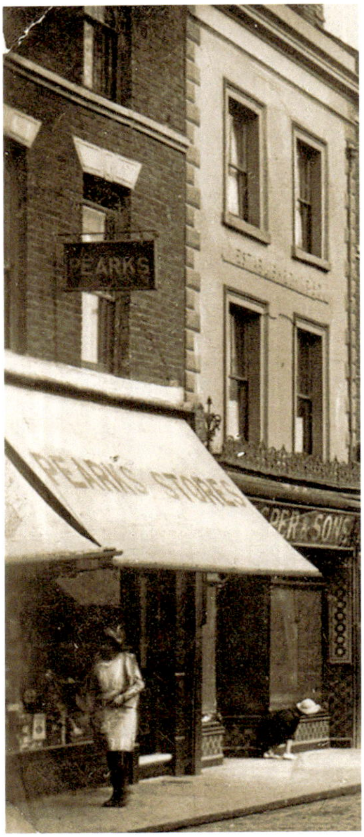

Two shops seen here in the early 1920s are Pearks' Dairies Ltd (No. 34 High Street) and Jasper and Sons Bakers (No. 36 High Street). Both enterprises continued trading at these same premises throughout the interwar years.

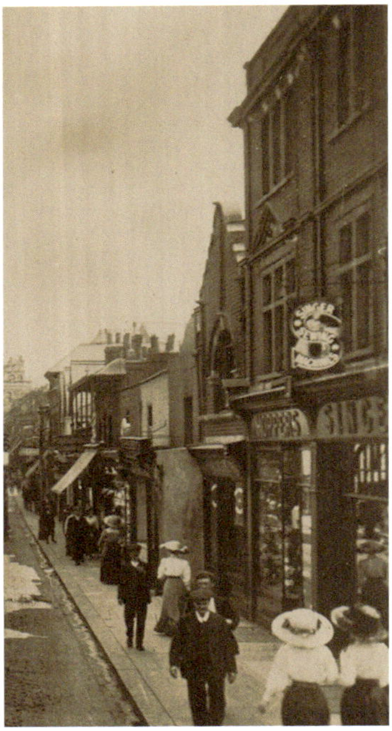

Going back to the years before the First World War, the shop in the immediate foreground is Singer Sewing Machines (No. 29 High Street), which continued to trade here for several decades.

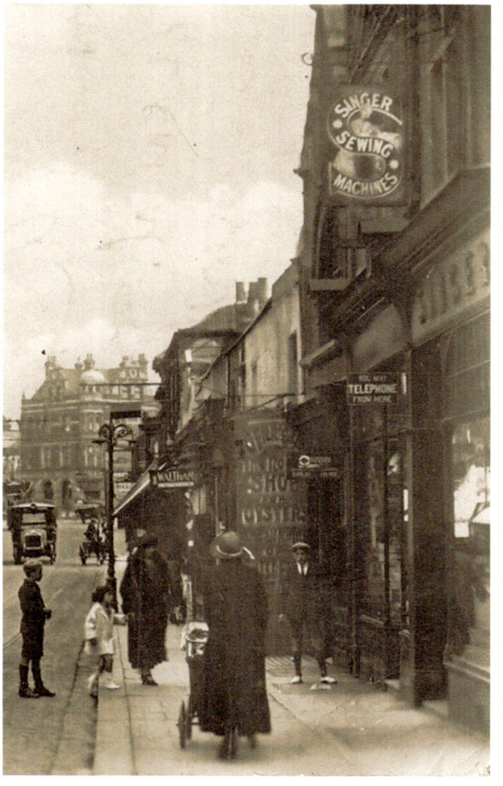

The same view (more or less) as the previous illustration but fifteen or more years later. Singer Sewing Machines is still there, while the shop just beyond is Fieldgate's, an oyster merchant (No. 31 High Street). Sandwiched between these two shops is A. E. Hornsby & Co., an electrical engineer selling Osram lamps (No. 29a High Street).

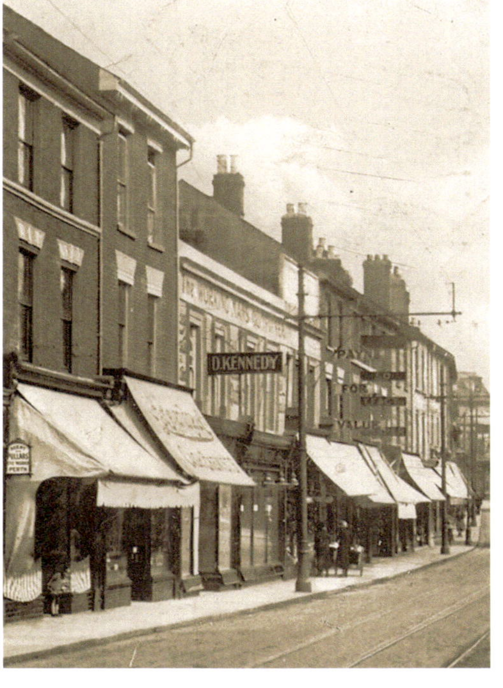

Another group of High Street shops captured here during the mid-1920s. Moving away from the camera are Beveridge & Co., chemist (No. 40 High Street), Kennedy Douglas, outfitters (Nos 42–44 High Street), J. Sears, bootmaker (No. 46 High Street) and Frank Payne, house furnisher (No. 48 High Street).

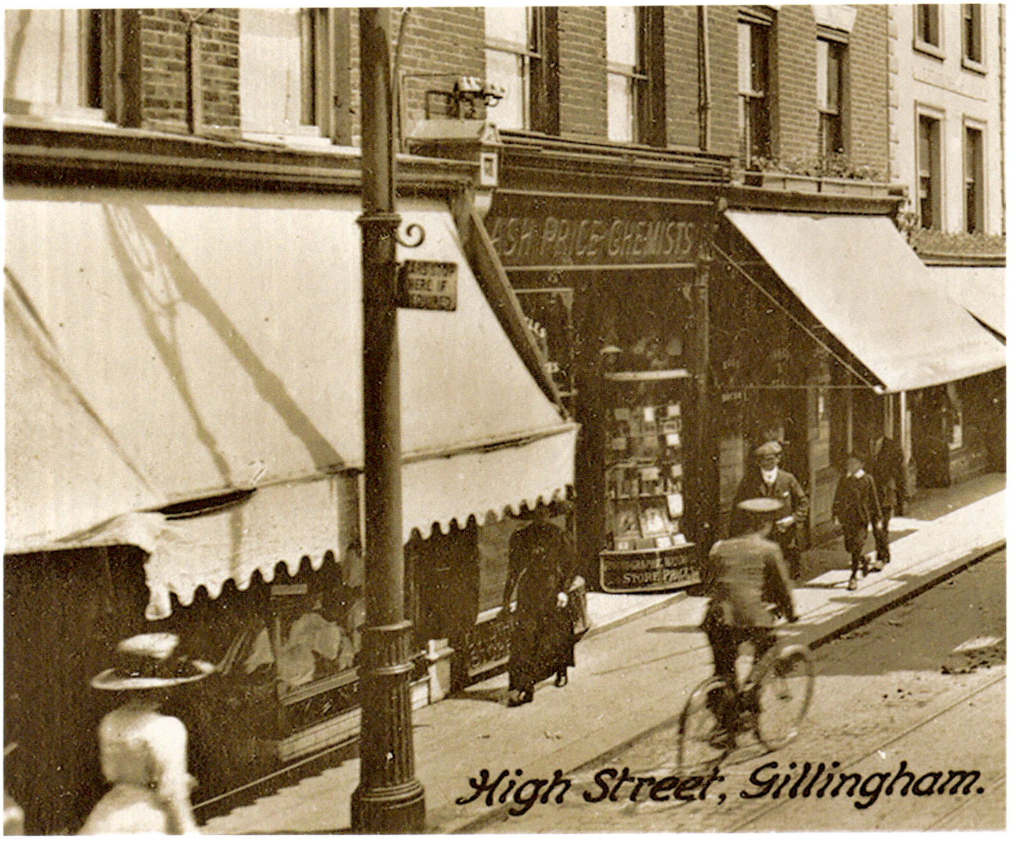

Seen here before the First World War, a soldier cycles past Beveridge & Co. (No. 40 High Street), the cash price chemist.

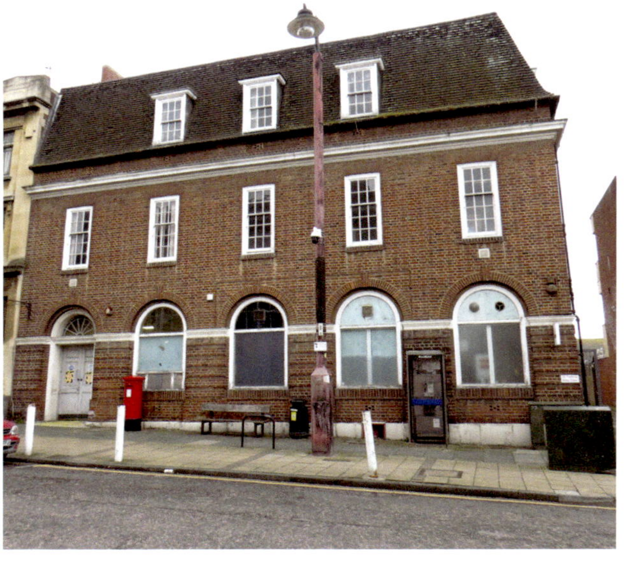

The former Post Office building in Green Street. First opened in 1926, it was a building designed by David Dyke.

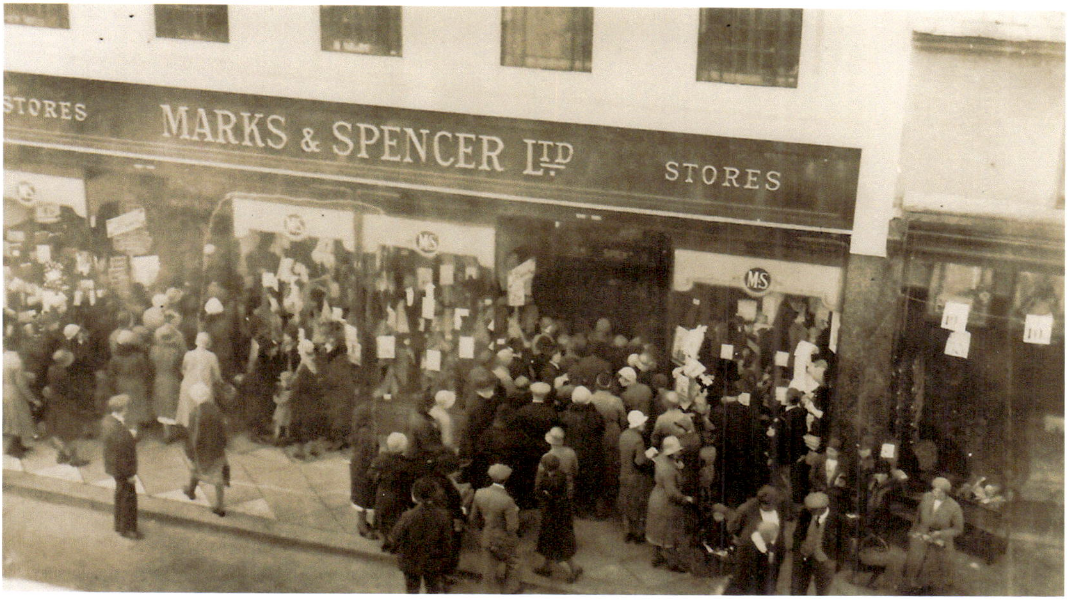

The opening, in October 1933, of a new Marks and Spencer store in the High Street (Nos 151–153 High Street). This replaced an earlier and much smaller store on the same site, which had first opened in July 1912, trading under the name of Marks and Spencer's Ltd., originators of Penny Bazaar. (Courtesy Marks and Spencer, plc)

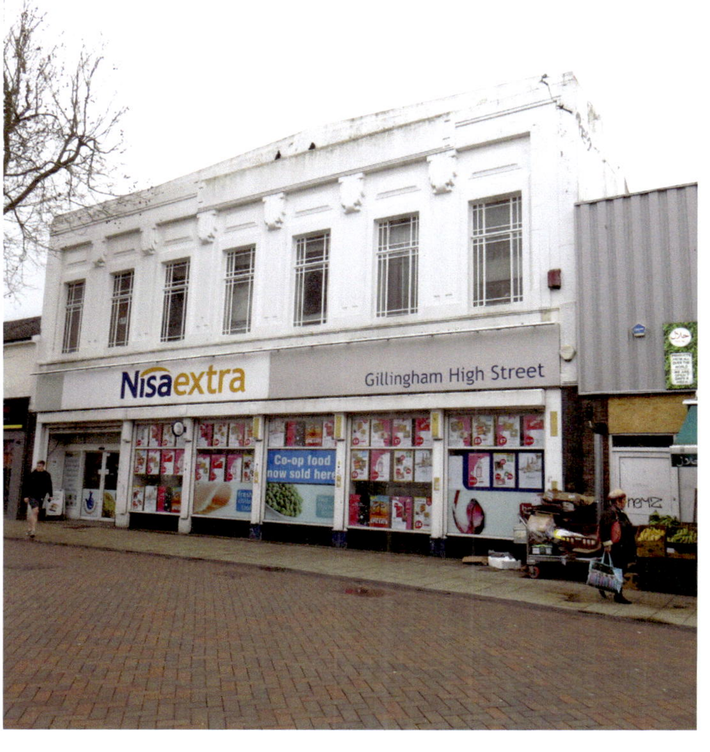

Today, the 1930s original Marks and Spencer building still exists, but is now in the possession of Nisaextra, a convenience store and small supermarket.

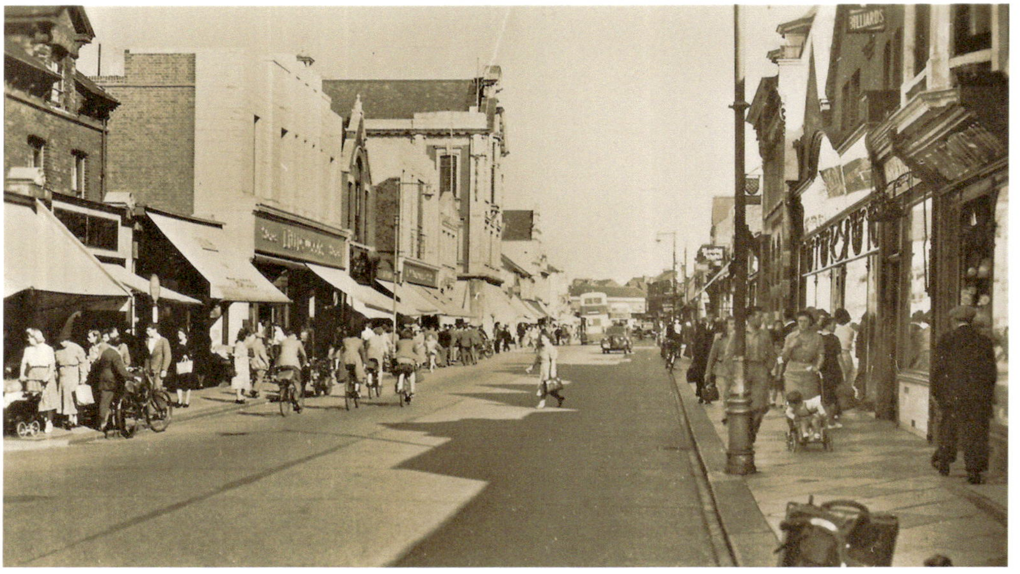

To be seen in this photograph, taken in 1949, is Littlewood's (Nos 118–120 High Street), another well-known high street store that no longer exists in Gillingham (nor elsewhere in the country). As a company Littlewood's became defunct in 2005. Beyond Littlewood's and just visible is the former premises of F. W. Woolworth (Nos 120–122 High Street), another one time giant of the high street. A point not to be missed is just how busy the High Street of Gillingham was during the mid-twentieth century.

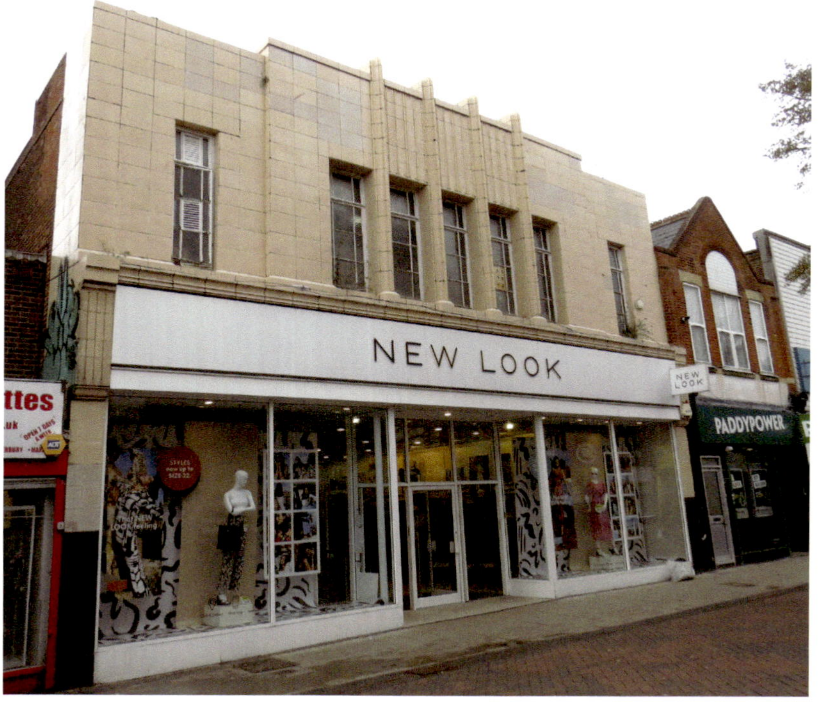

The building that was once a Littlewood's store is still to be seen but is now a New Look fashion retailer.

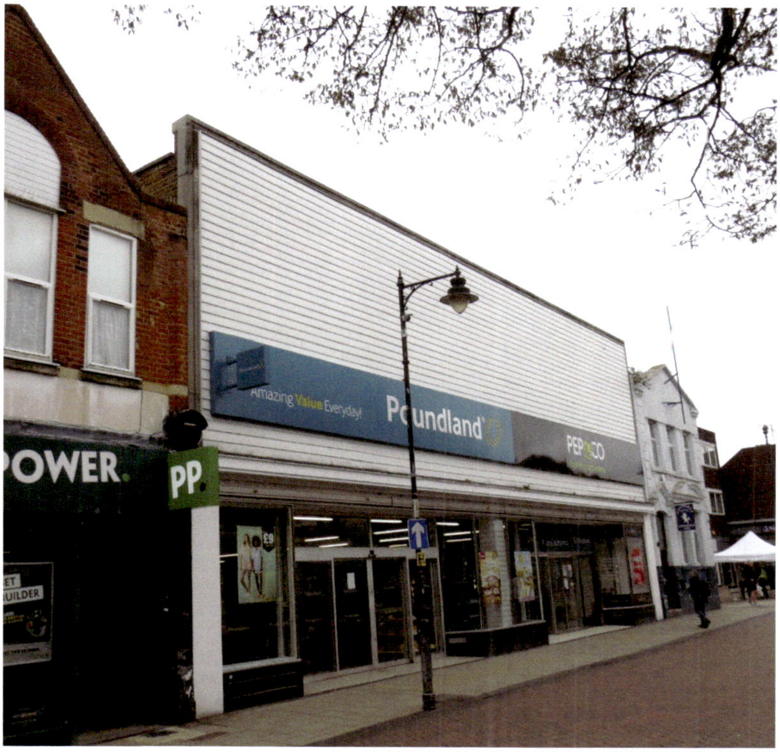

Similarly, the building once occupied by F. W. Woolworth, affectionately known as 'Woollies', is still present. Following the closure of this Woolworth's branch in 2008 the store first became a 99p store but is now Poundland. In 1971 the Gillingham store was given an industrial-style façade made of reinforced plastic panels, with the present-day Poundland store reflecting that later makeover rather than the earlier corporate style that Woolworth's had once adopted.

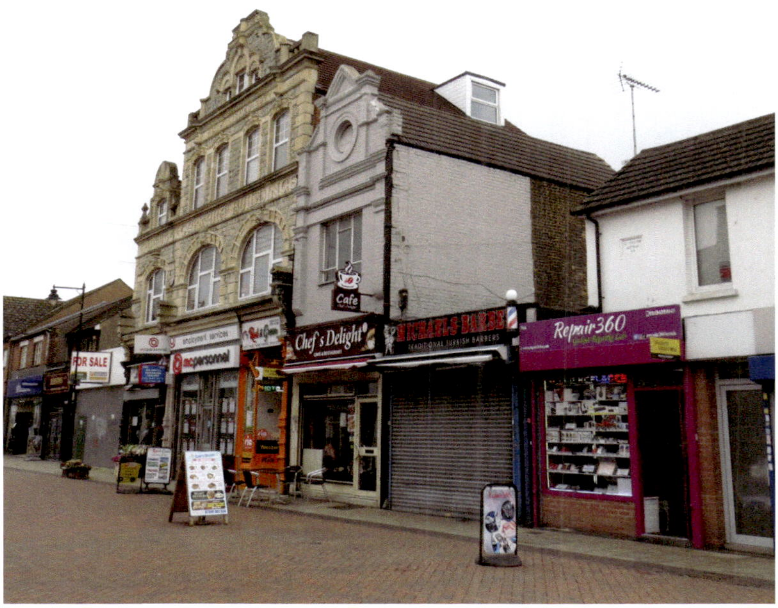

A view of the High Street as it is today. The major part of it is pedestrianised, making it a much more pleasant shopping space, but shopping by way of the internet means it has less visitors and thought needs to be put towards saving and reinvigorating the heart of the town.

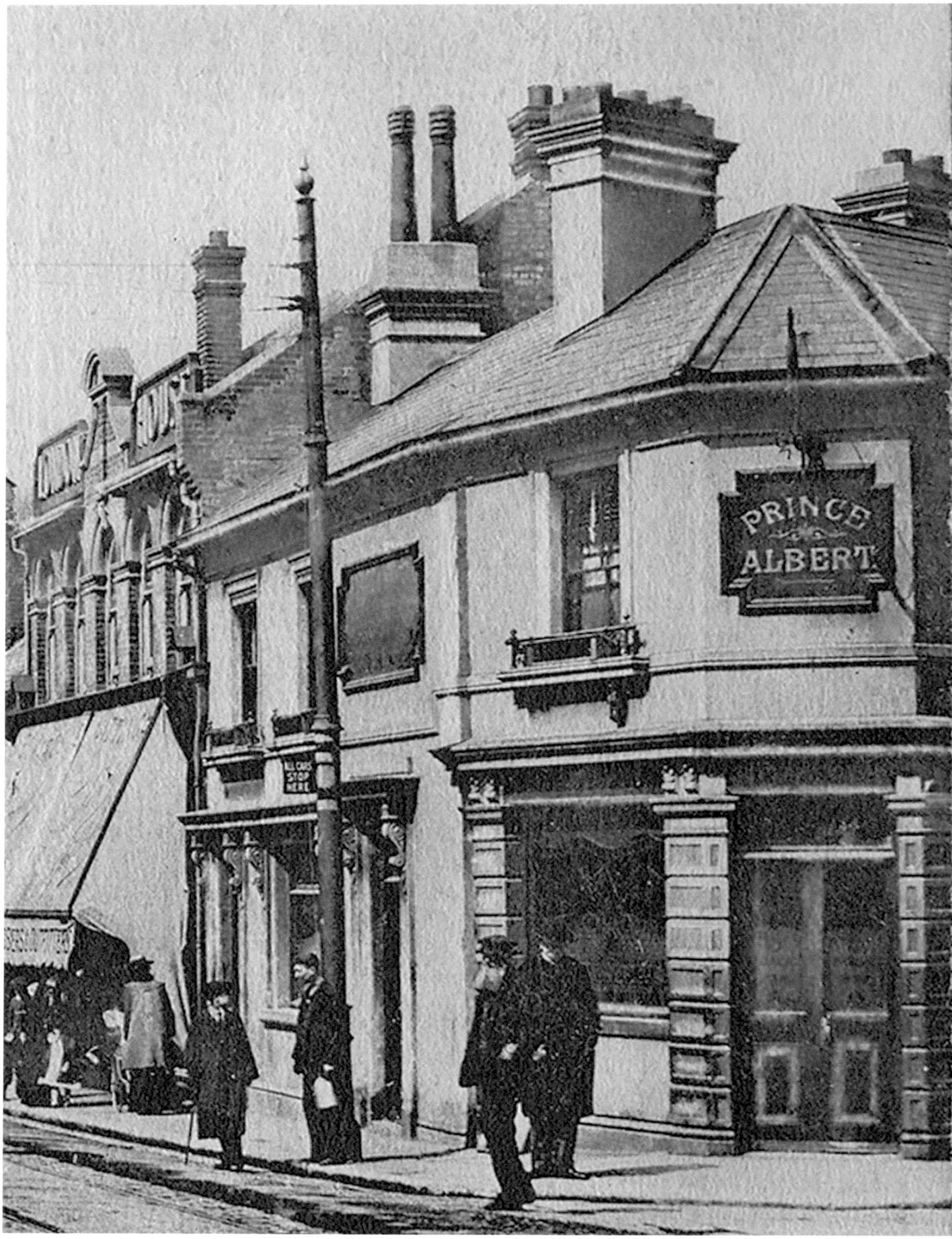

The Prince Albert (No. 80 High Street) seen here *c.* 1910. This pub opened during the 1870s and was popular with those who came to Gillingham seeking work in the dockyard.

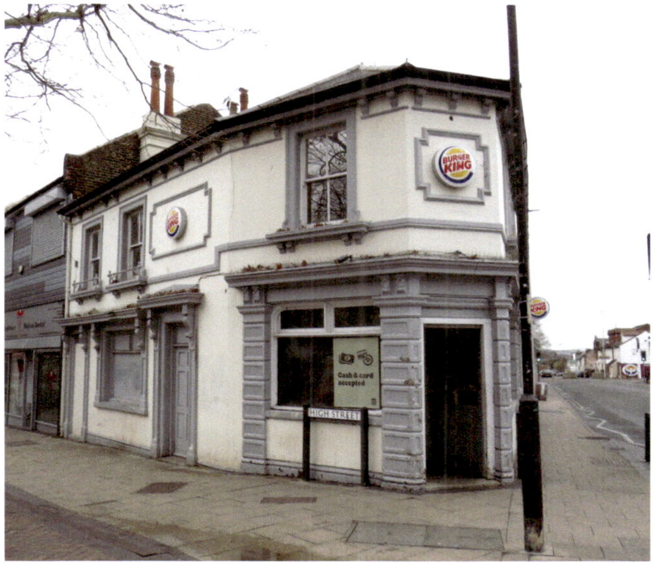

No naval or military town would be complete without places of entertainment, but especially pubs to quench the thirst of off-duty servicemen and those working in the dockyard. Gillingham, of course, was no exception, with the High Street during the 1920s boasting eight pubs or other establishments selling alcohol. One pub that has not survived is the Prince Albert on the corner of Skinner Street, today a fast-food restaurant.

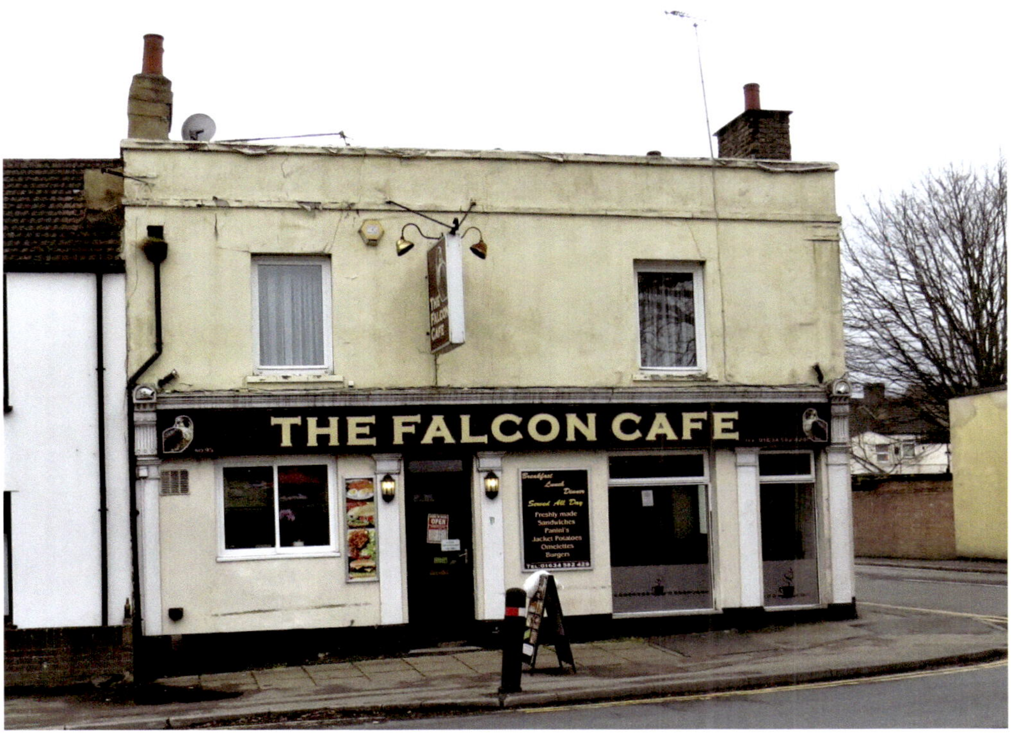

Another pub that has failed to survive is the Falcon (No. 95 Marlborough Road/formerly Park Place), which dated back to at least 1848 when the landlord was a Paul Skelton. In those days, being on the edge of the Lines and close to various naval barracks, it would have been popular among those who had taken the 'King's Shilling'. Closed in 1995, it is now a café but retains the name of the former pub.

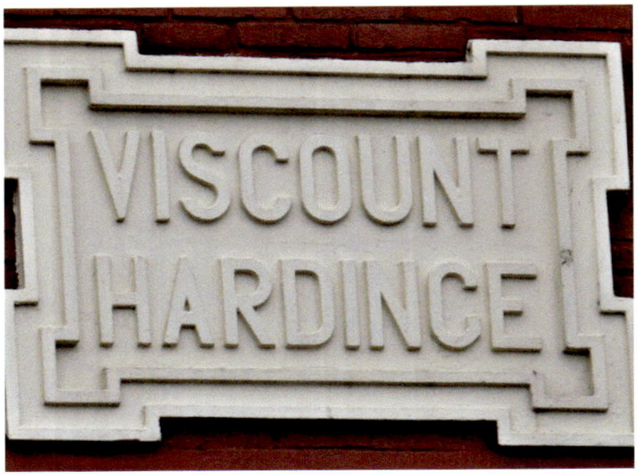

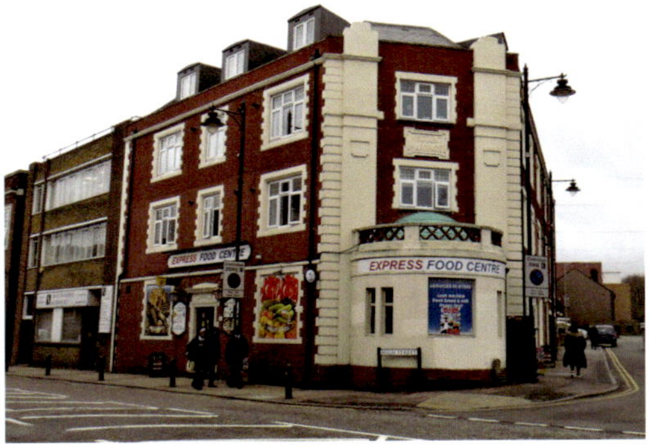

Now an Express Food Centre, the Viscount Hardinge (No. 3 High Street) first opened as a public house sometime in the 1840s and finally closed in 2011. At one time it was renamed the Lord Hardinge, before later returning to its original name. The first Viscount Hardinge was Commander-in-Chief of the Forces during the Crimean War, accompanying both Queen Victoria and Prince Albert when, in June 1855, they visited soldiers wounded in the Crimea who were recovering in both St Mary's Barracks and a supplementary hospital established in Brompton Barracks. Seemingly, in 1909 the Viscount Hardinge, due to being an up-market establishment, was the one pub in Gillingham that could, when Christmas day was not on a Sunday, remain open.

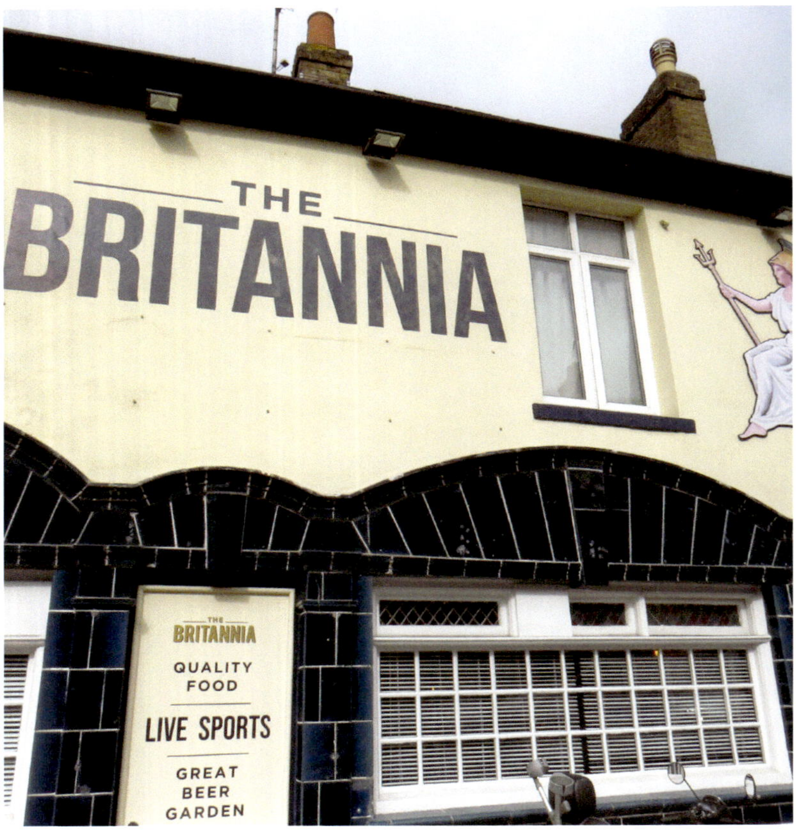

One of many still surviving pubs in Gillingham is the Britannia (No. 158 High Street), which goes back to the early 1860s, a time when New Brompton, as it was then known, was beginning to see a population surge as a result of the dockyard extension.

The nineteenth-century Westcourt Arms in Gillingham is seen here following a snowstorm in March 1909. Now permanently closed, the Westcourt Arms suffered serious fire damage in 2021.

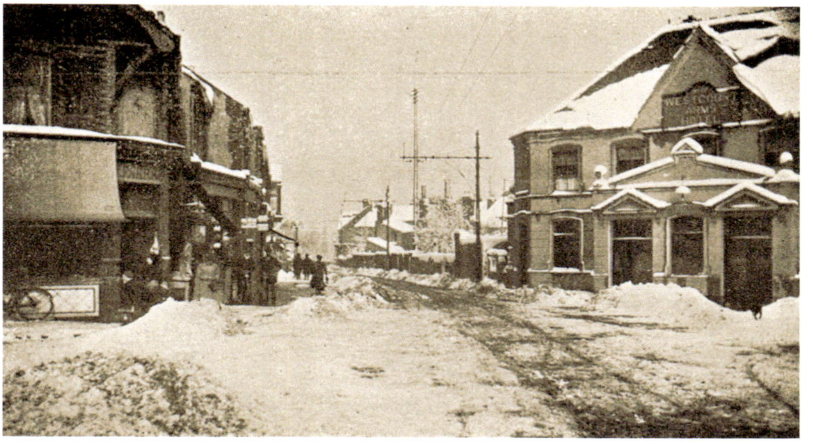

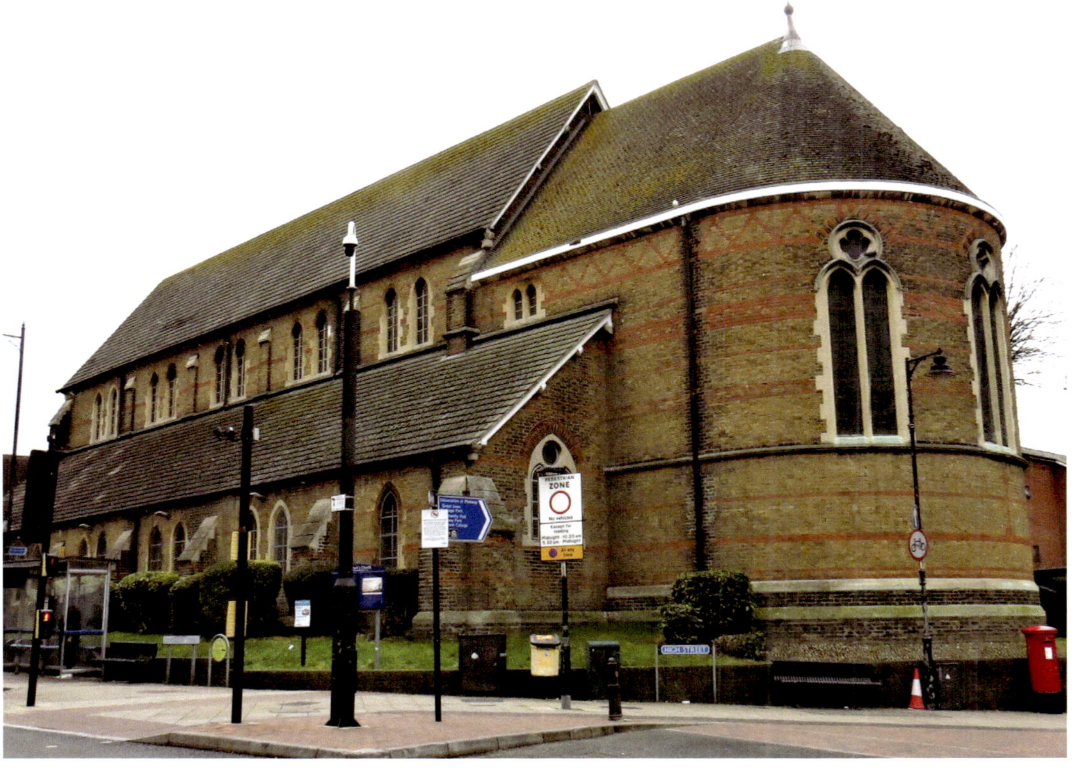

St Mark's Church, Canterbury Street. Consecrated on 24 April 1866 by George Murray, the then Bishop of Rochester, the opening of this church filled a massive vacuum in the lives of those who worshipped in the established church. The community growing in and around New Brompton was some distance from the parish church on the Green, with St Mary's in Chatham no closer. It was therefore decided to create a new parish to be served by a new and sizeable church. This was St Mark's, with construction of the church commencing in 1864. The estimated cost of constructing the church was £8,000 and the land on which it stands was purchased for £237.

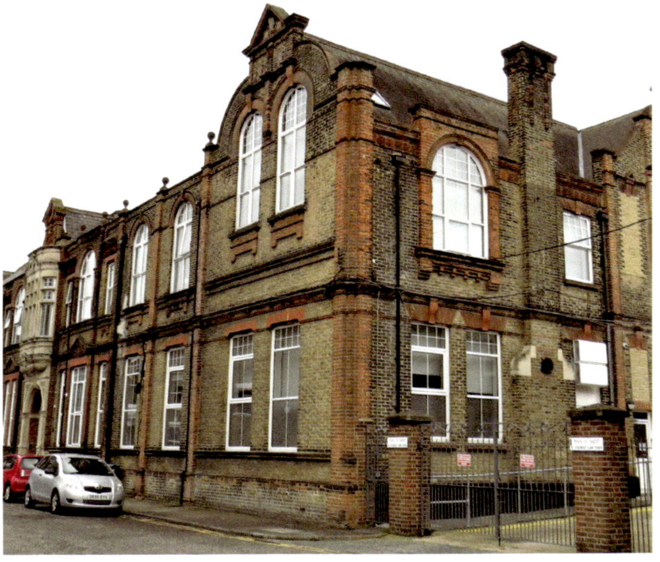

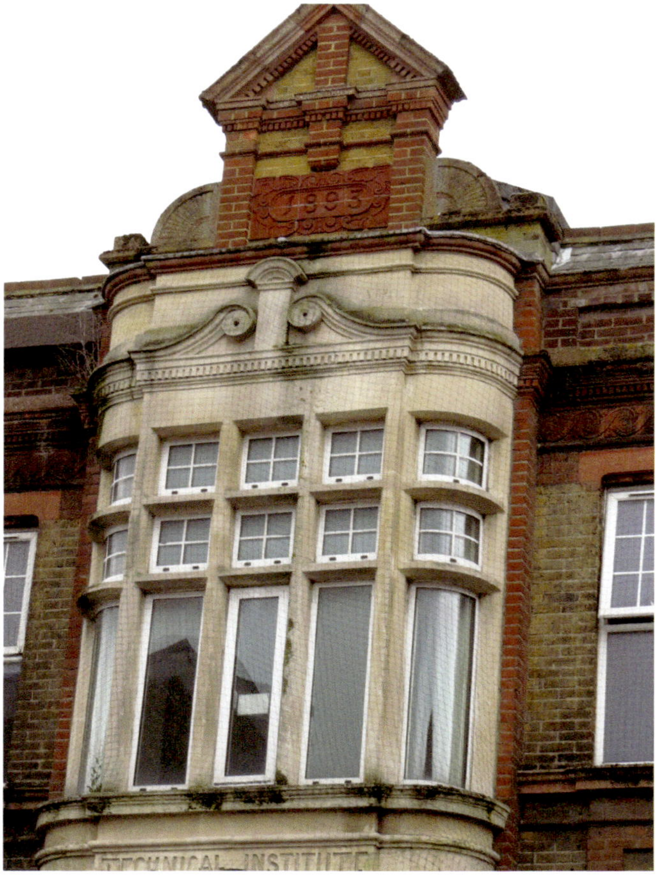

This building in Gardener Street still stands, with its original purpose emblazoned on the front façade in stone – Technical Institute. It was completed in 1894 at a cost of just over £2,000 and designed by G. E. Bond of Rochester. Bond was the designer of a number of fine buildings across the Medway Towns. In later years it became a Technical School, part of the tripartite system of education introduced after the Second World War, with overflow classes held upstairs in the Odeon cinema (originally the Gem and later the Embassy), which was adjacent.

7

Family Entertainment

With so many families moving into New Brompton during the second half of the nineteenth century, a need was created for local entertainment that the entire family could enjoy. To meet that need, a combination of enterprising individuals and the subsequently formed town council set about ensuring that those who lived in the borough had access to a range of wholesome activities that would satisfy most tastes.

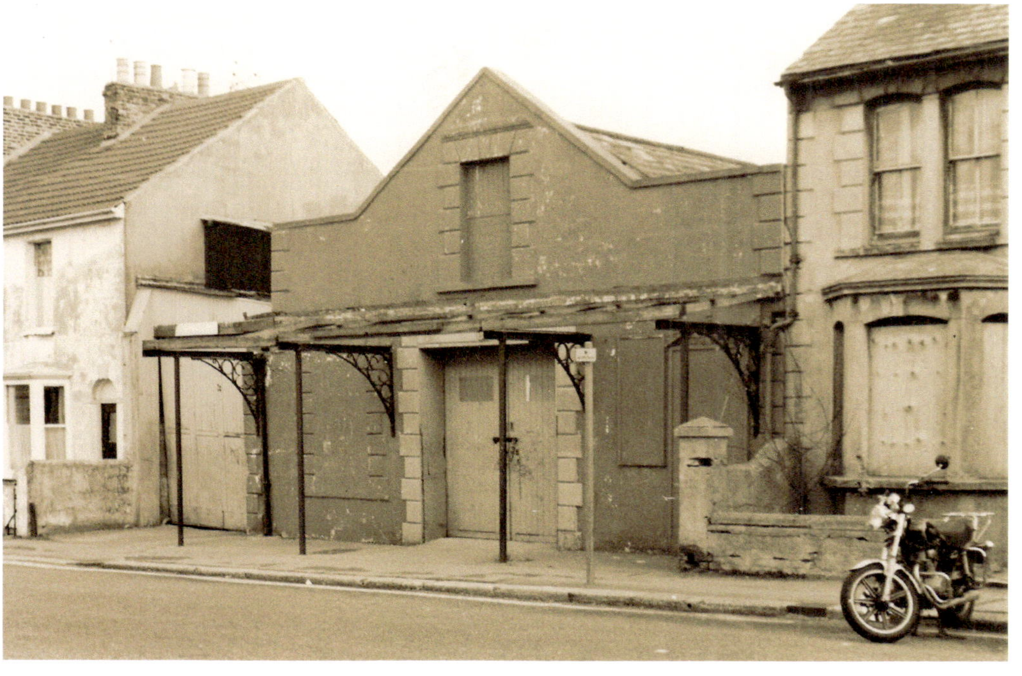

Opened in January 1910, the Gem Variety Theatre' in King Street (later the King's Hall) was an early venue for the showing of films; at first only short films intermingled with stage acts. One early popular film shown shortly after the opening of the Gem was scenes of a football match played between New Brompton and Norwich. A sound system was introduced in 1930, but five years later a fire destroyed much of the cinema, although the building itself survived (but now demolished), with this photograph taken in 1987.

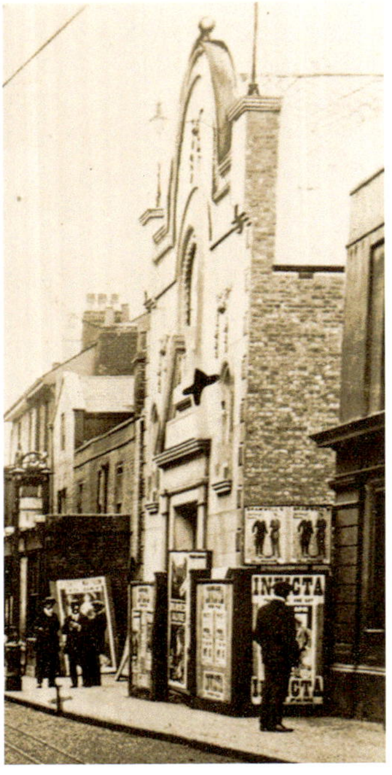

The Invicta Picture Palace in the High Street shortly after its opening in early 1914. Situated immediately next to the Viscount Hardinge public house, in common with that pub it was owned by the Croneen family, an influential local family. The Croneens, during the nineteenth century, had wisely invested in land in this part of Gillingham, also establishing a jewellery shop (Nos 21 and 23 High Street), which, as can be seen from where this photograph was taken, stood on the far side of the 'Invicta'. As for the cinema itself, this was built of bricks manufactured by another Croneen enterprise, a brickfield owned by the family.

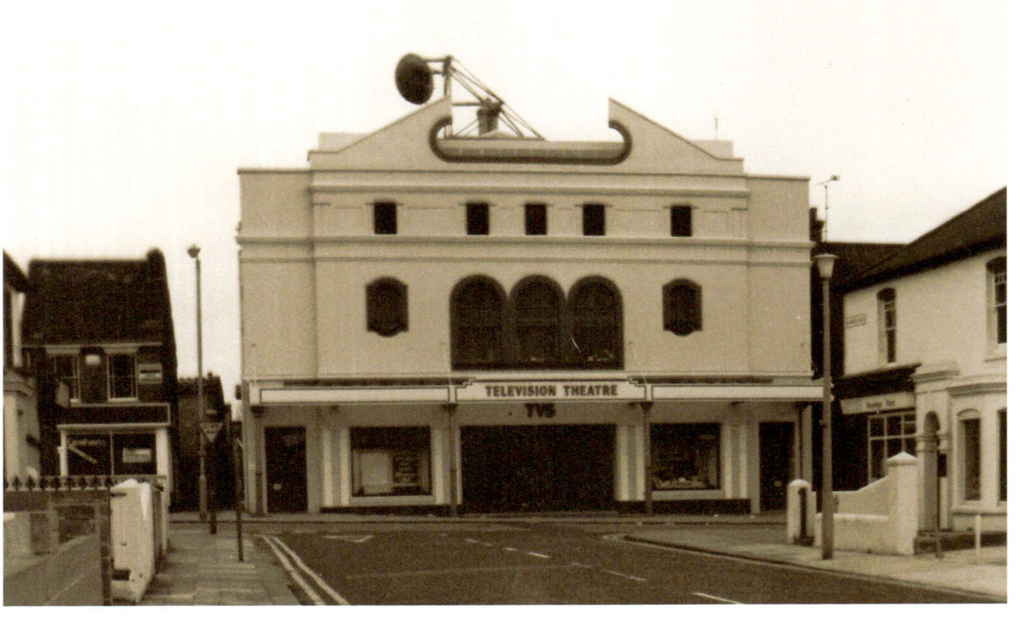

The 'Invicta' continued to screen films until 1931 when the Croneen family, on land owned in Duncan Road, opened a much larger cinema. This was the 1,804-seater Plaza Super Cinema (No. 70 Duncan Road), which first began screening films in October of that year. While it was not the first cinema in the Medway Towns to show 'talkies', it was the first to have a sound system built into its original design. The Plaza continued showing films until 1980, but is seen here in 1987 when it had been adapted to the needs of a local television station.

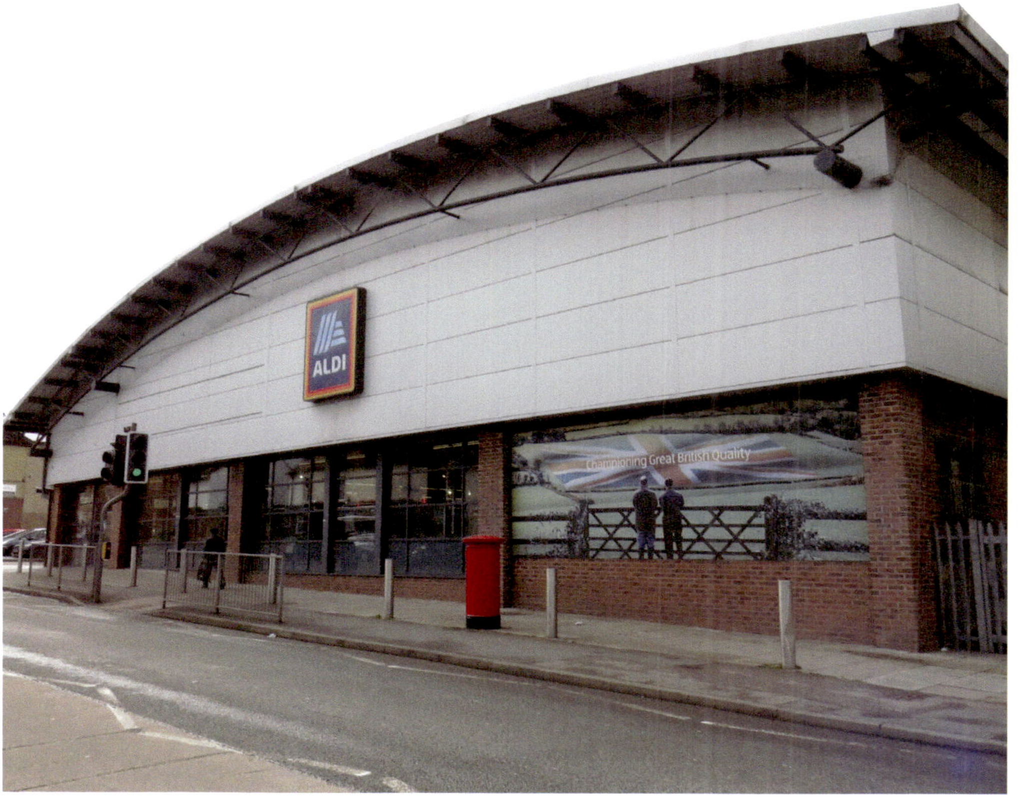

The Plaza is no more. It has been demolished and replaced by an Aldi supermarket.

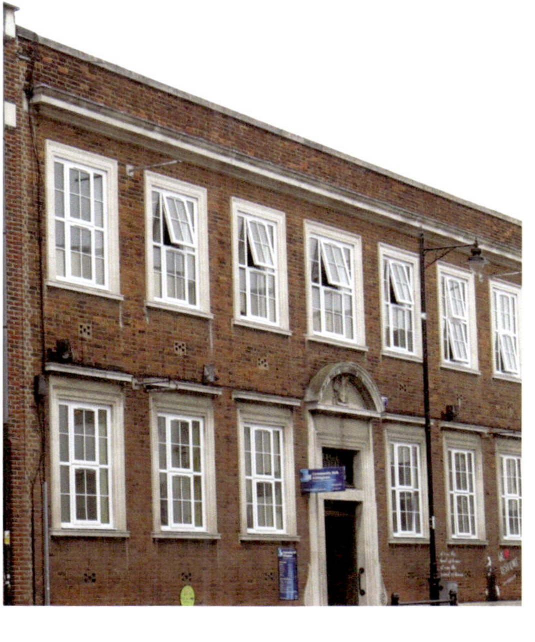

As for the original Croneen cinema, the Plaza in the High Street, this also has long ceased to exist. As a building it remained for many years, empty to begin with and then taken over by Wallis Motors Ltd, a motor car agency. Here, in this picture, the site of the old Plaza cinema is occupied by a new building squeezed in between the library and the Viscount Hardinge.

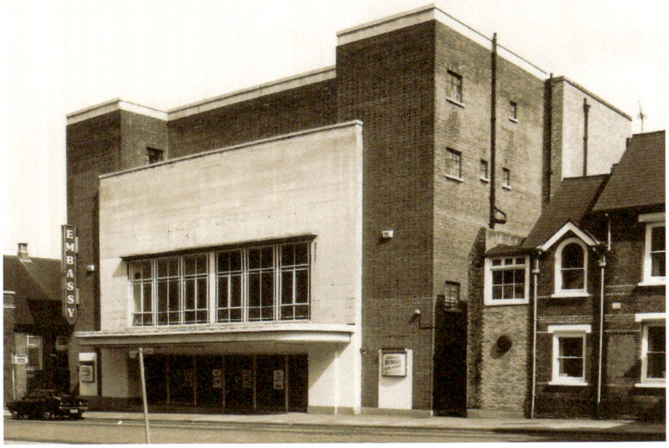

The Embassy in Gardiner Street, seen here in 1987, was, at the time of its opening on 3 October 1936, considered a luxury cinema that was meant to be part of a much grander scheme that would have seen part of Gardiner Street developed into an upmarket shopping area. However, it was a concept that got no further than the opening of the cinema.

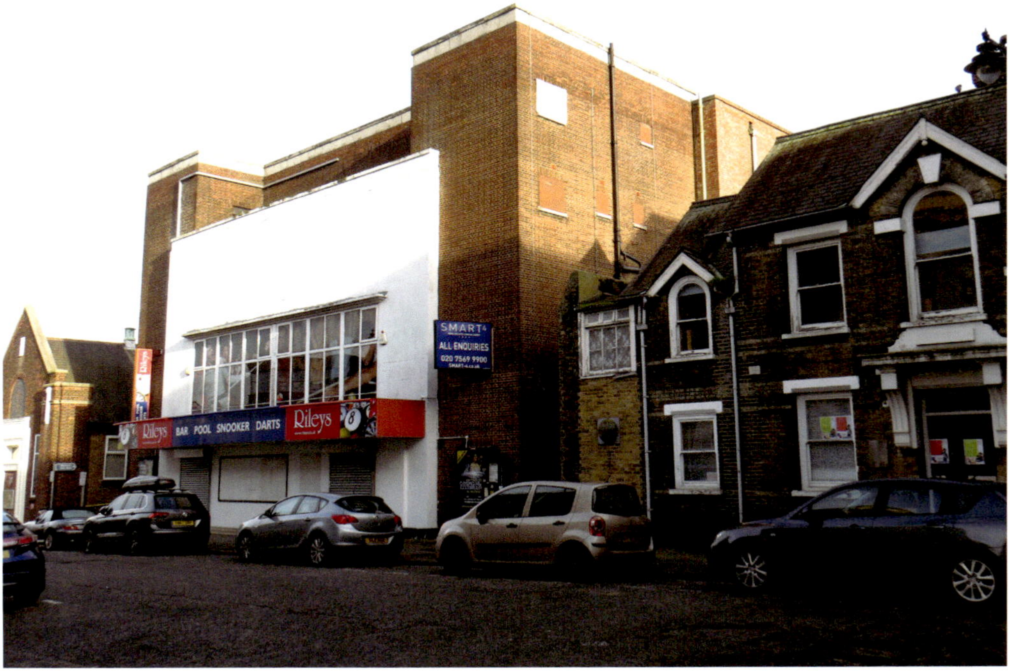

A much more recent photograph of the original Embassy. This cinema was the creation of Bertie Garrett, the former owner of the Gem cinema, who had decided to open a new cinema for Gillingham following the fire that had brought an end to the screening of films at the Gem. As an independently owned cinema the Embassy had a short life, joining the Odeon circuit just a few years after its opening.

Another film venue, if only occasionally, was the Salvation Army hall in Green Street, where films were sometimes shown on Saturday mornings for children, which were free and intended to provide an alternative to the Saturday morning films shown almost next door at the Odeon. The building itself dates to 1934 and was opened on 7 April of that year, but the Salvation Army's connection with Gillingham dates back to 1881 and the formation of the New Brompton Corps.

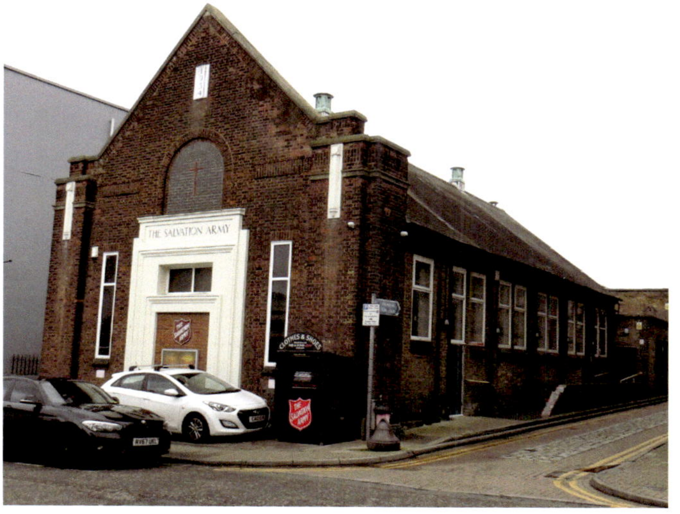

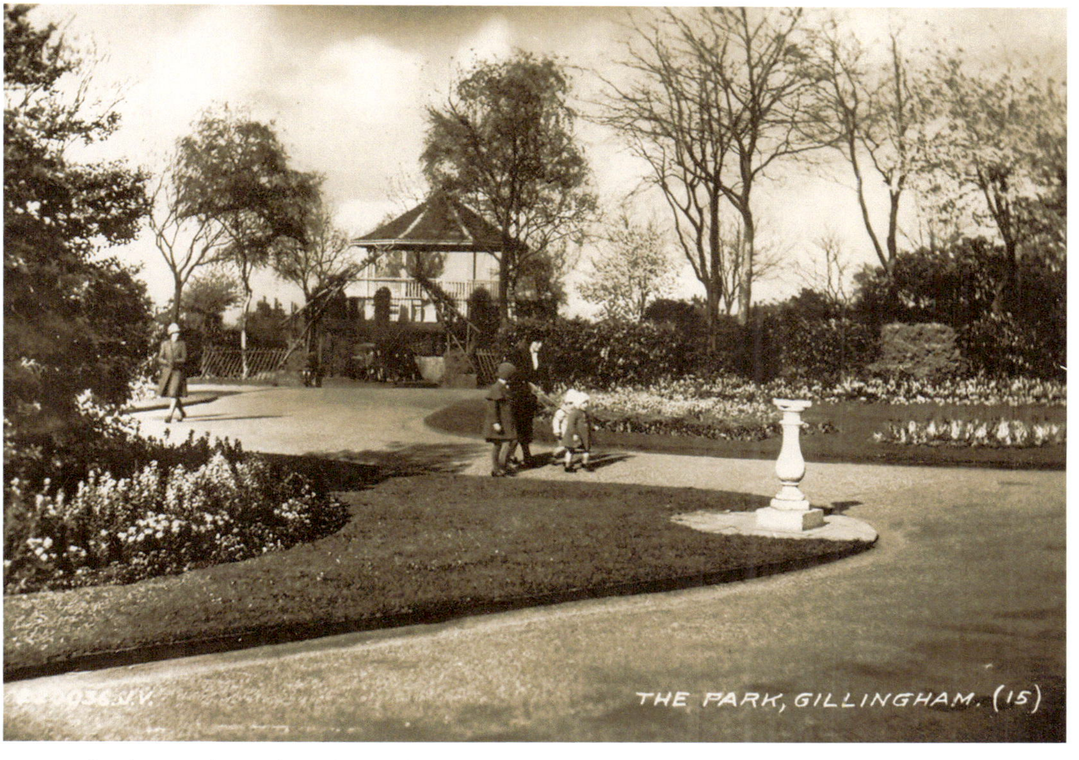

Gillingham Park seen here during the late 1920s. Opened in July 1906, work on laying out the site had begun two years earlier, with the park covering an area of 16 acres. As for the bandstand (a feature no longer present), this saw the holding of regular afternoon concerts, although at one time these were restricted to Wednesday and Saturdays as concerts on Sunday, being the 'Lord's Day', were banned.

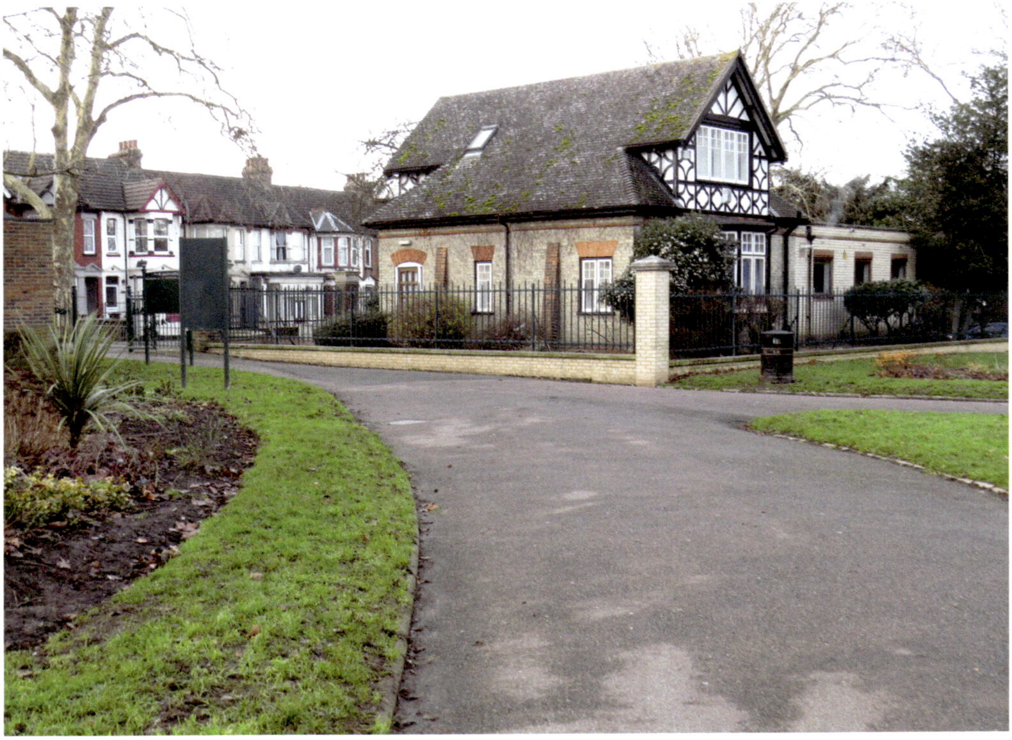

The park entrance today. Unfortunately, during the summer of 1929 Gillingham Park witnessed an awful tragedy when a regular display, held each year by the fire service, went terribly wrong. A three-storey temporary structure, known as the 'Hot Villa', instead of emitting red smoke to resemble a fire, and from which a family were to be rescued, burst into actual flame, with those who should have been rescued, some fifteen in number, unable to escape.

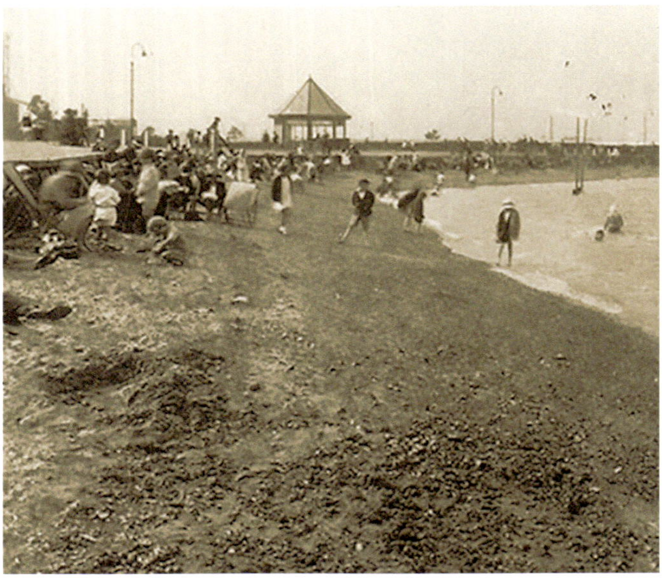

The Strand, Gillingham's very own beach, continues to be a popular summertime resort for residents, but much more so in earlier years when holidays to foreign parts were a rarity. The development of this river frontage came about during the 1890s when Thomas Cuckow, a local baker, opened a swimming pool in June 1896, situated just above the high water mark.

A late 1920s photograph of the Strand that is strangely entitled 'enjoying the sun'. Judging by the choice of clothing worn that day, there was little sun, appearing more like a typical pre-global warming English summer's day.

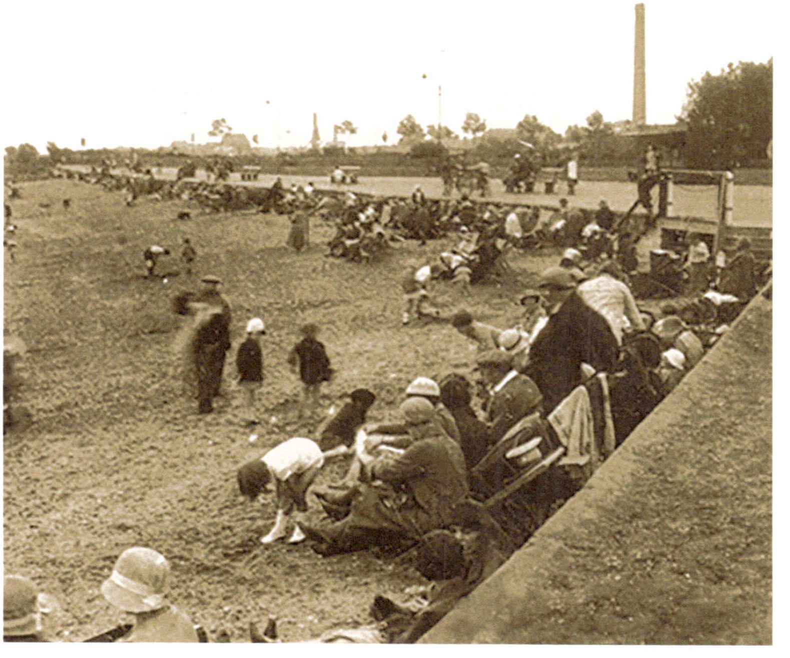

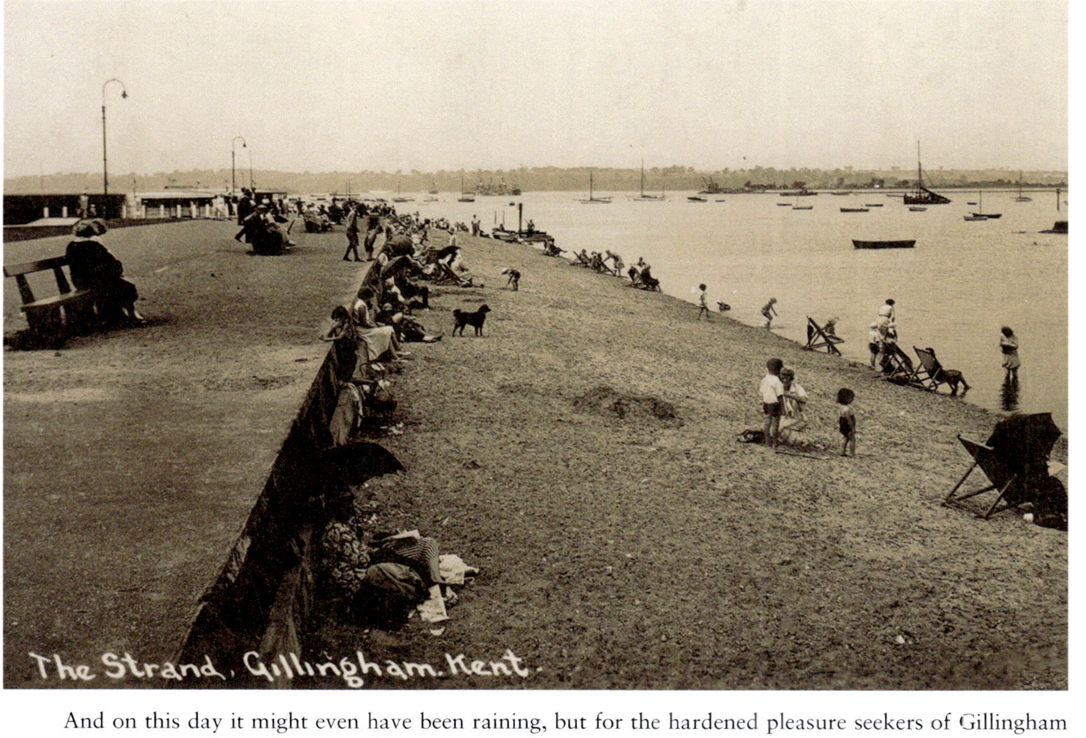

And on this day it might even have been raining, but for the hardened pleasure seekers of Gillingham this was no real problem – just bring an umbrella!

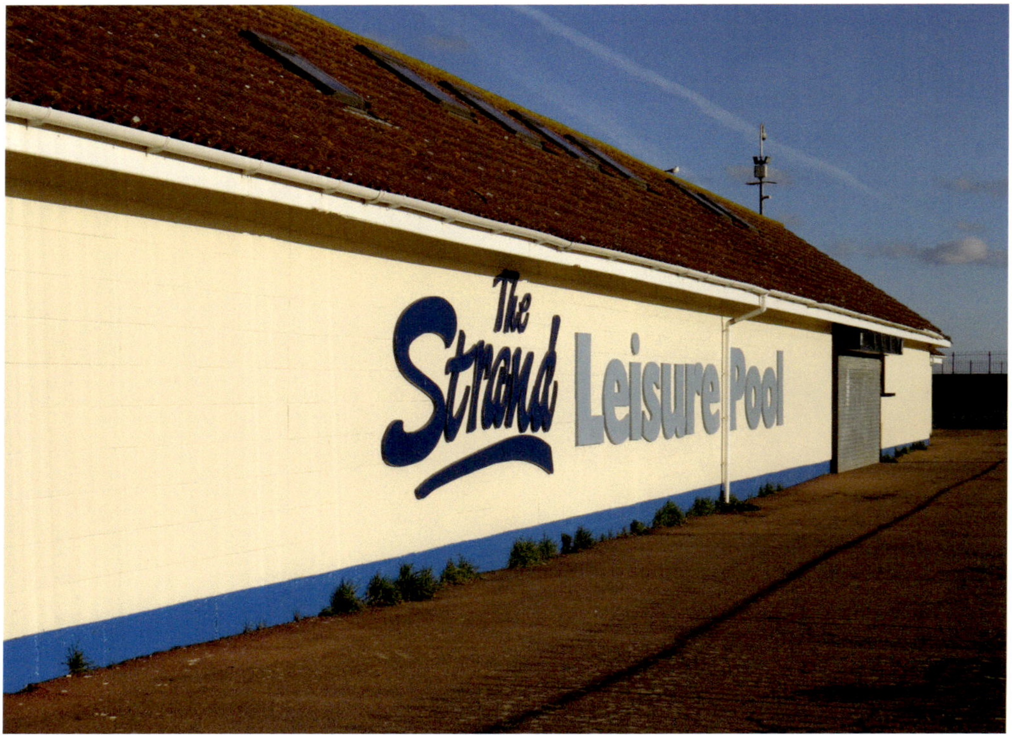

The open-air swimming pool acquired chlorination and filtration units together with wooden changing rooms in the 1920s. In the hands of the borough council, a paddling pool, bandstand, car park, ice cream parlour and deck chairs were also added at this time. Of course, many further improvements have since followed including the frequent updating of the children's' play park and the introduction of a miniature railway line.

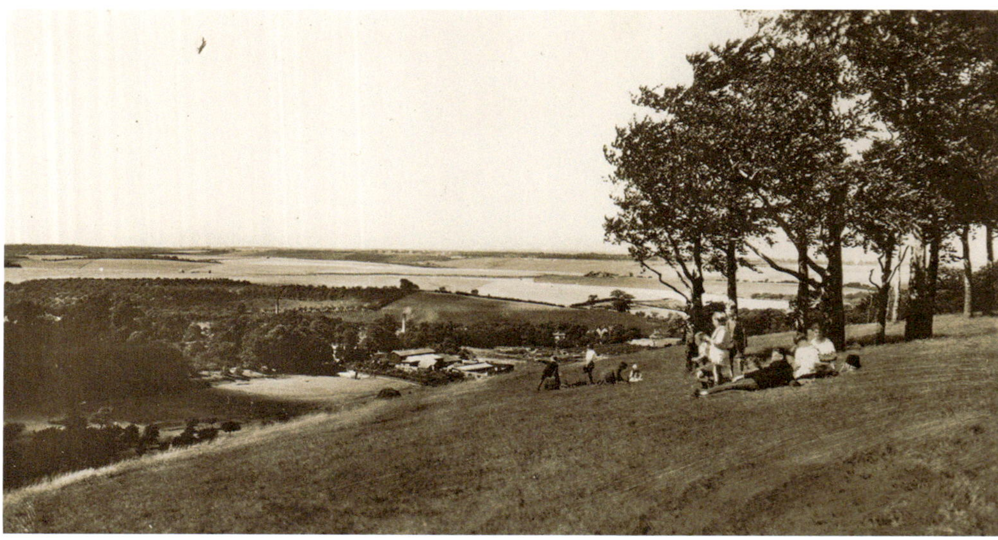

The delights of Darland Banks seen here during the interwar years.

8

Memories

Memories are very personal; what one person remembers of Gillingham may well be very different to those of another. Much of this book is doubtless steered by my own memories of the town, developed during the time I lived there (the 1970s and 1980s). To begin with, it was still a town influenced by the Royal Navy and the dockyard. Some residents feared that closure of the yard was a possibility, many more believed otherwise. After all, to help secure work in the yard it had seen the addition of the nuclear refit facility, an essential asset for maintaining the Navy's hunter-killer submarines. The crane that towered over the facility there for all to see. Yet closure did happen, and this, in particular, shaped my experience of living in Gillingham. First, Navy Days, a major annual event, followed by the cancelling of the last of those Navy Days because of the Falklands War, then the close-down ceremony, which was followed in turn by an all-pervading sense of gloom that completely engulfed the town and many of its long-term residents.

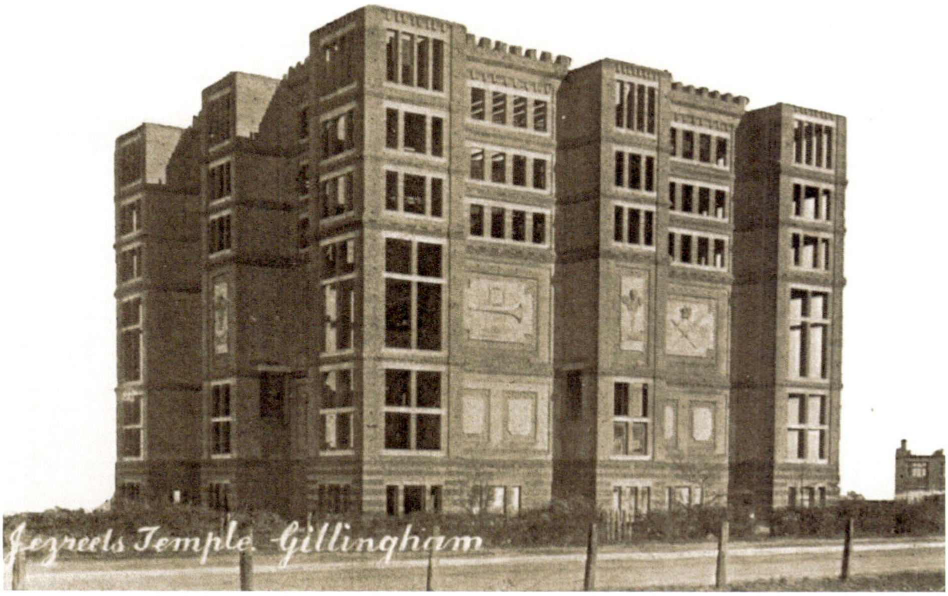

Gillingham once possessed a truly mysterious landmark visible for miles around: a giant cube-like structure adorned with motifs and projecting turrets that offered few clues as to its purpose or origin. Roofless, with unglazed windows, it stood on ground sided by Rainham Road to the south and Canterbury Street to the east. For residents travelling back to Gillingham by road, whether from one of the seaside resorts in East Kent or a business trip to London, an early glimpse of the tower, often from some distance, was a sure and comforting sign that home would shortly be reached and the day's journey was coming to a close. This was Jezreel's Tower.

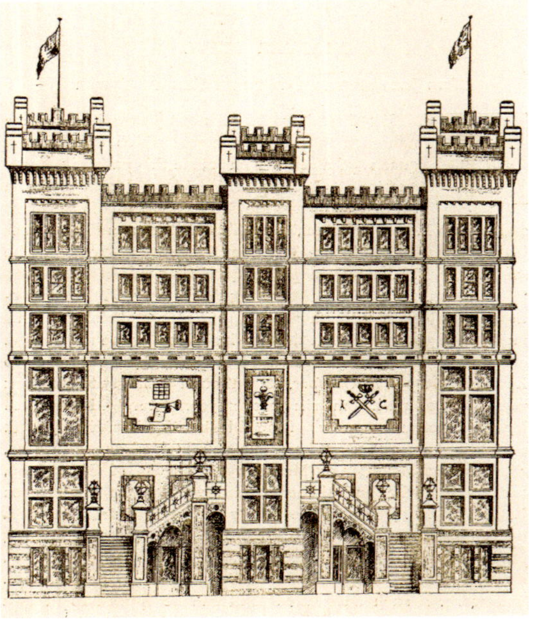

Jezreel's Tower was never completed to its final design. This picture shows how it would have appeared if the money had been there. Announcing that it was through a dream that God had commanded him to build the tower, James Jershom Jezreel (real name James Rowland White), the founder of a religious sect known as the Jezreelites, said that it should, in appearance, replicate the shape of Jerusalem as described in the Book of Revelations.

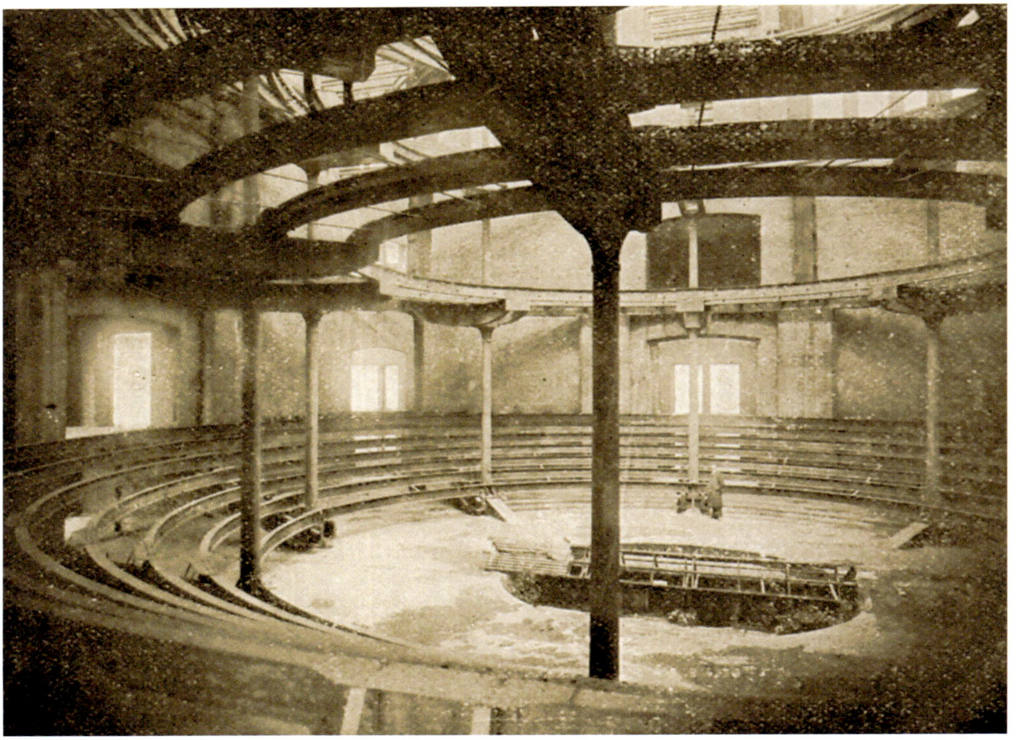

The central assembly room of Jezreel's Tower seen sometime around 1905. The area in the centre was intended to feature a hydraulically powered platform that would have been raised from the floor below and on which preachers and a choir could be accommodated.

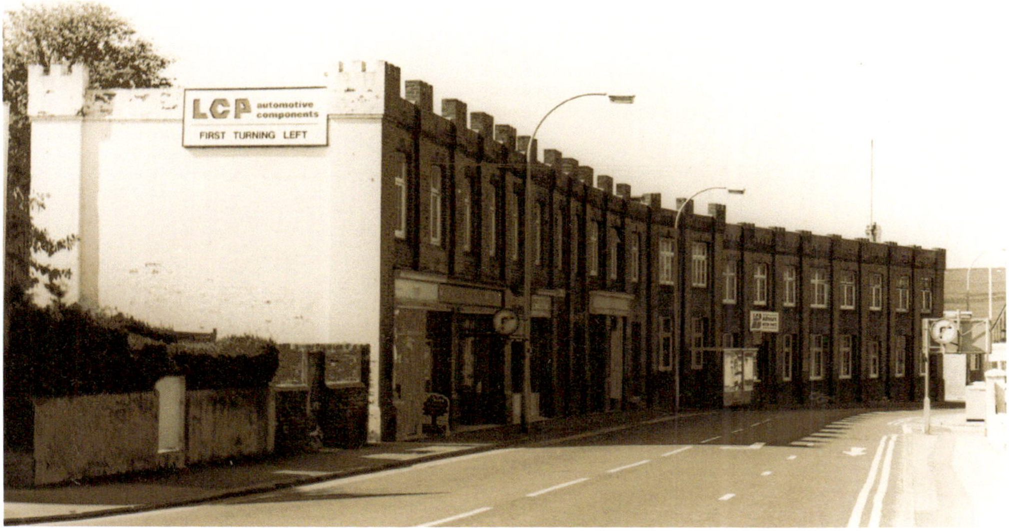

A further group of buildings once owned by the sect lined the top end of Canterbury Street, but they were demolished in 2008. Built in 1886, they were originally used for instructing scholars in the 'true' faith.

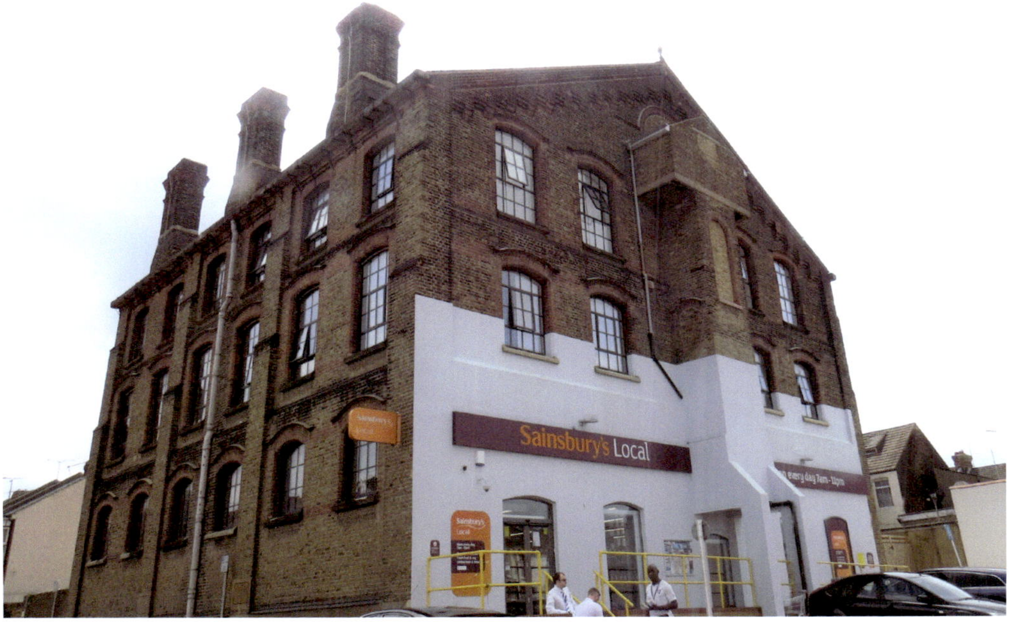

This building (No. 277 Gillingham Road) has a unique history. It was built for an early cooperative group, the New Brompton Economical and Providential Society, which was once separate from the wider co-operative movement as established in Rochdale in 1844. In fact, the co-operative movement in the Medway Towns goes back much further, workers in the dockyard establishing a co-operative system during the late eighteenth century, purchasing produce wholesale and selling to members at close to cost price. The New Brompton Society, again by those employed in the dockyard, was established in 1867 for the bulk buying of food.

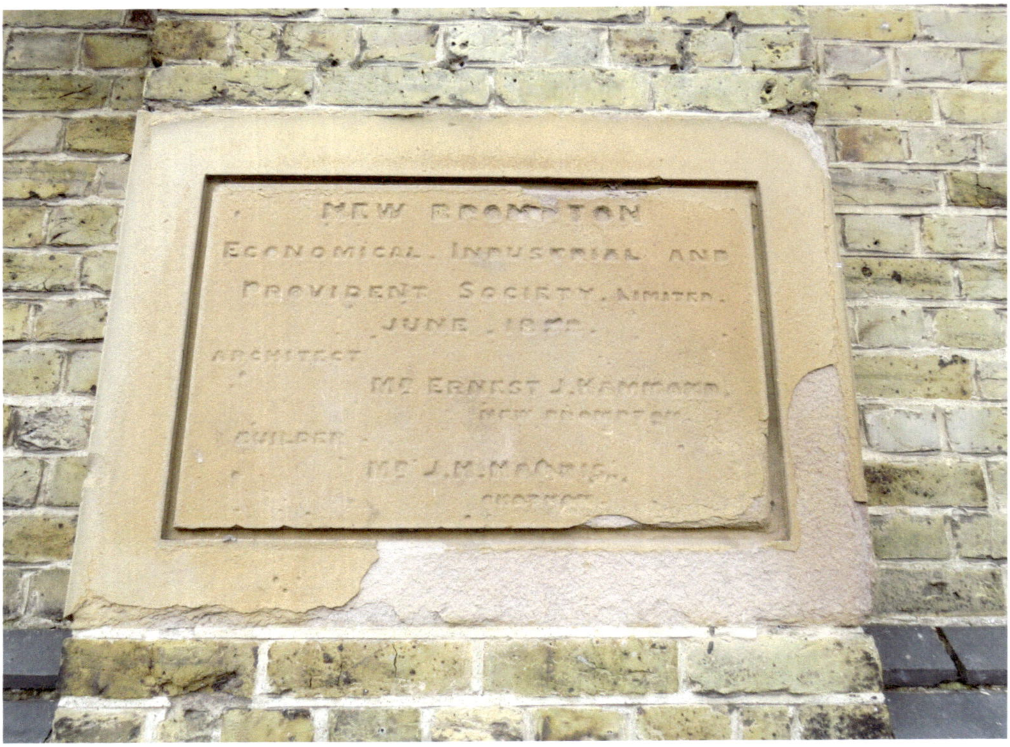

From the time of its formation in 1867, the New Brompton Economical and Providential Society met with great success, able to not only construct the building in Gillingham Road, where this plaque is to be found, but also to establish a number of other shops in the town. In time, the New Brompton Economical and Providential Society was absorbed into the national co-operative movement, but with the shop in Gillingham, once a co-operative store, now a Sainsbury's Local.

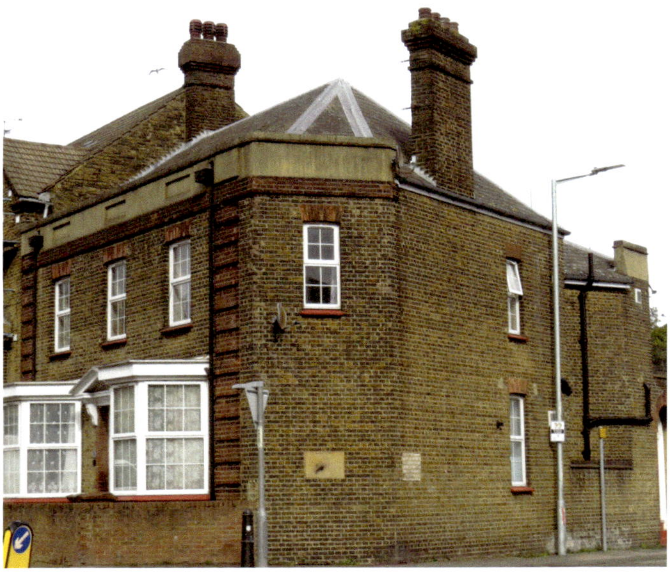

This house on the corner of Kingswood Road and Station Road was once the premises of the Gillingham Invicta Benefit Medical Society, a benefit society that predated the National Health Service, continuing until the formation of the NHS, whereby members paid in a weekly sum of money which ensured that they would receive medical treatment without the need for additional payments.

This plaque can still be found on the side of the premises formerly belonging to the Gillingham Invicta Benefit Medical Society.

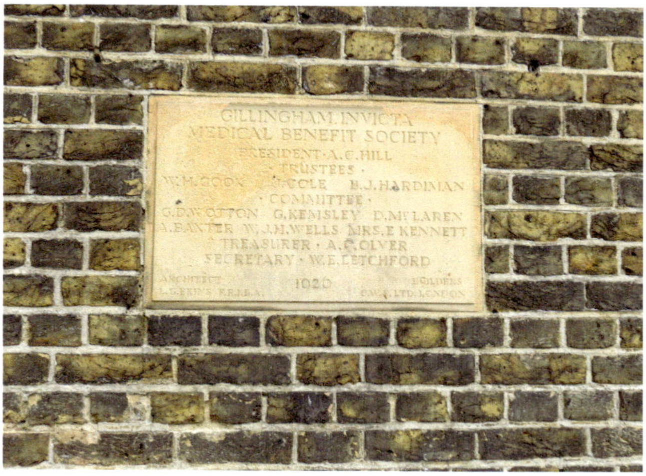

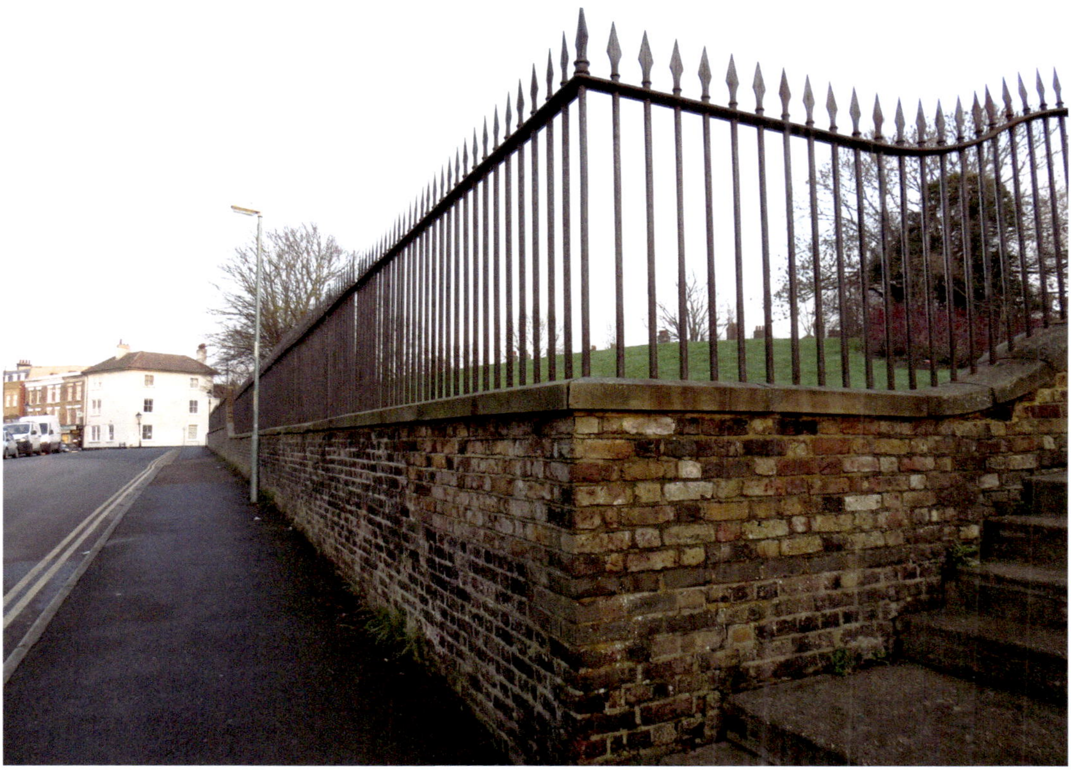

The wall of this park, which fronts on to Garden Street in Old Brompton, has a unique history Dating to 1827, it once enclosed a reservoir that contained up to 500 tons of water and was built by the Admiralty to provide water for Melville Hospital, the old naval hospital that stood where Melville Court is now located. It had been thought water might have been pumped from a reservoir in the dockyard, but this would have required considerable use of the dockyard steam pumps to get the water to the necessary height, with this reservoir having only to rely on gravity for the flow of water to the hospital, which was on a level beneath Old Brompton.

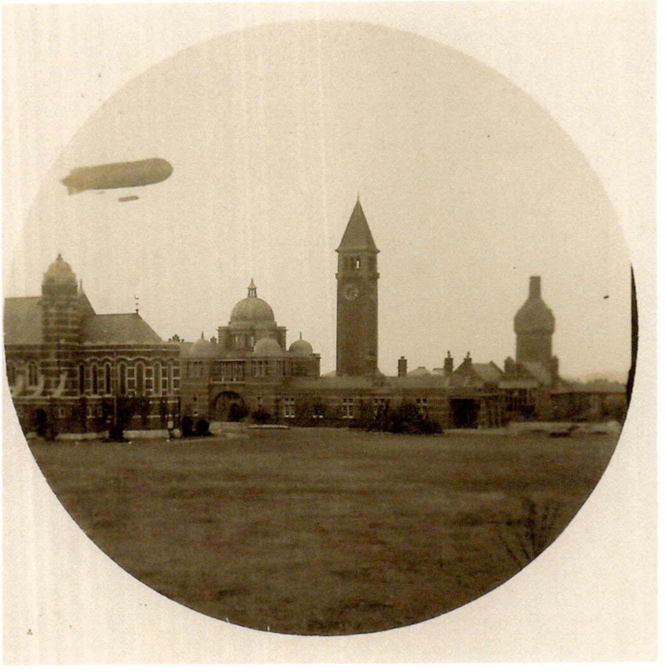

In 1914, when this photograph was issued and turned into a postcard, the sight of any kind of aerial craft, in this case a Royal Navy airship, was something strange and unusual. The airship seen here, *Delta*, is passing over the Royal Naval Hospital (now Medway Maritime), having just been acquired by the Royal Navy from the Army. It was probably based at Kingsnorth where a naval airship station had been established.

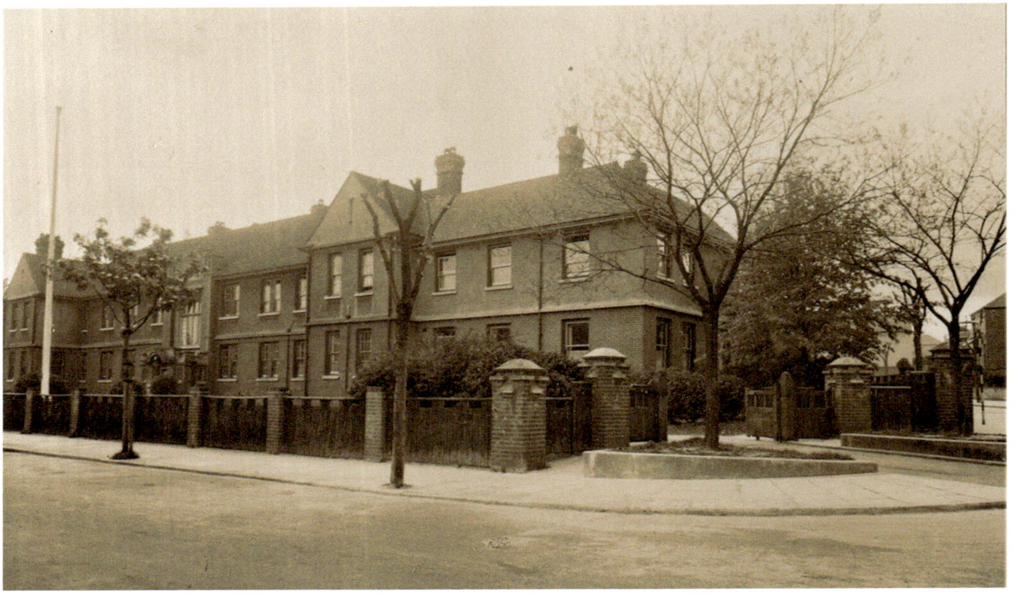

Canada House, Royal Navy and Marine Maternity Home, Barnsole Road (between Alexandra and Larkfield avenues), seen here *c*. 1925. During the First World War a house was established in Franklin Road to care for the wives of servicemen about to give birth, with Canada House, after the war, taking on this role. It was named Canada House as some of the funding was donated by the Canadian government and it was opened by Princess Marie Louis, a granddaughter of Queen Victoria, on 22 November 1922.

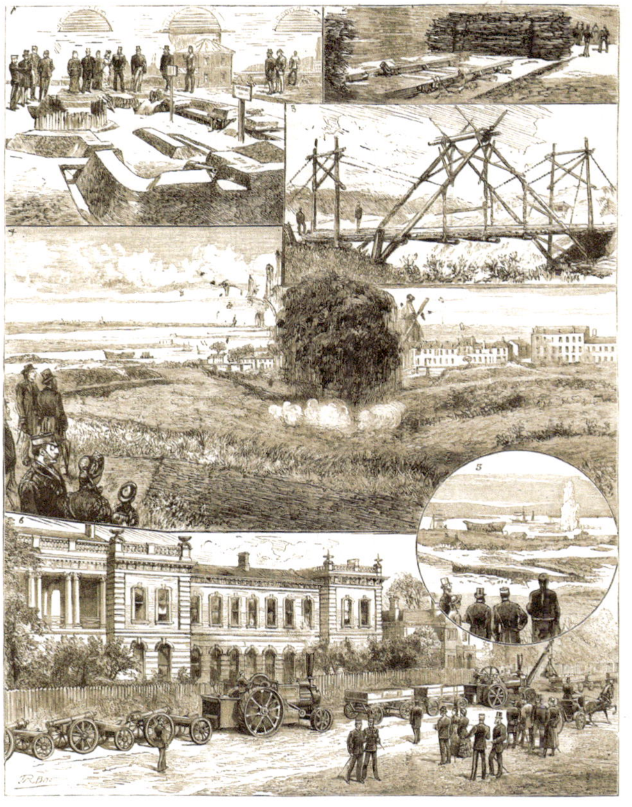

Various sketches made of the School of Military Engineering within Old Brompton RE Barracks and which appeared in the 4 November 1882 issue of *The Graphic*. These pictures show, from top left clockwise: types of field redoubts to resist light field Artillery, demolition of a railway, a treble-sling bridge, a mine of attack fired by a charge equal to 1,000 lbs of powder, explosion of a submarine mine in the Medway off Gillingham and procession of steam sappers before the school.

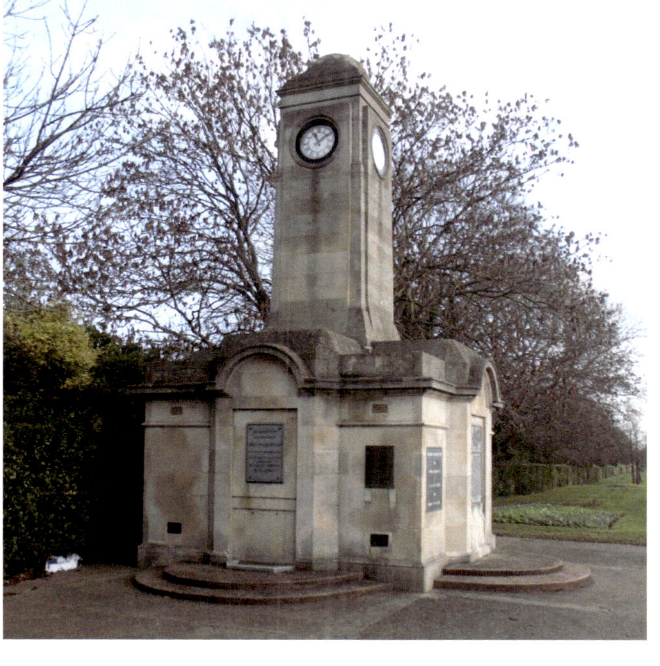

Gillingham has long been proud of its connections with Will Adams, the sixteenth-century seaman who, so it is claimed, was the first Englishman to set foot in Japan. Overall, little is known of his early years other than that, at the age of twelve, he was apprenticed to Nicholas Diggens of Limehouse, learning the intricacies of seamanship and gaining a Trinity House navigators licence. The memorial on Watling Street that commemorates his life was unveiled in 1934.

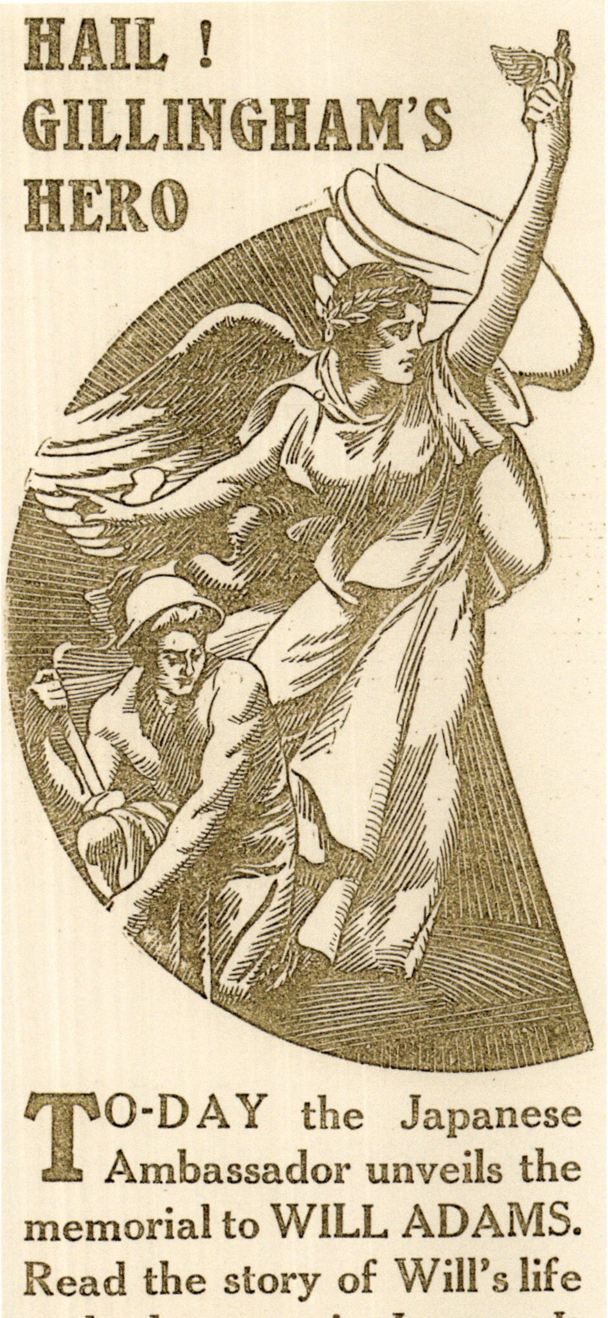

To coincide with the unveiling of the Will Adams memorial one local newspaper, the *Chatham Observer*, produced a special booklet which it advertised in the manner seen here.

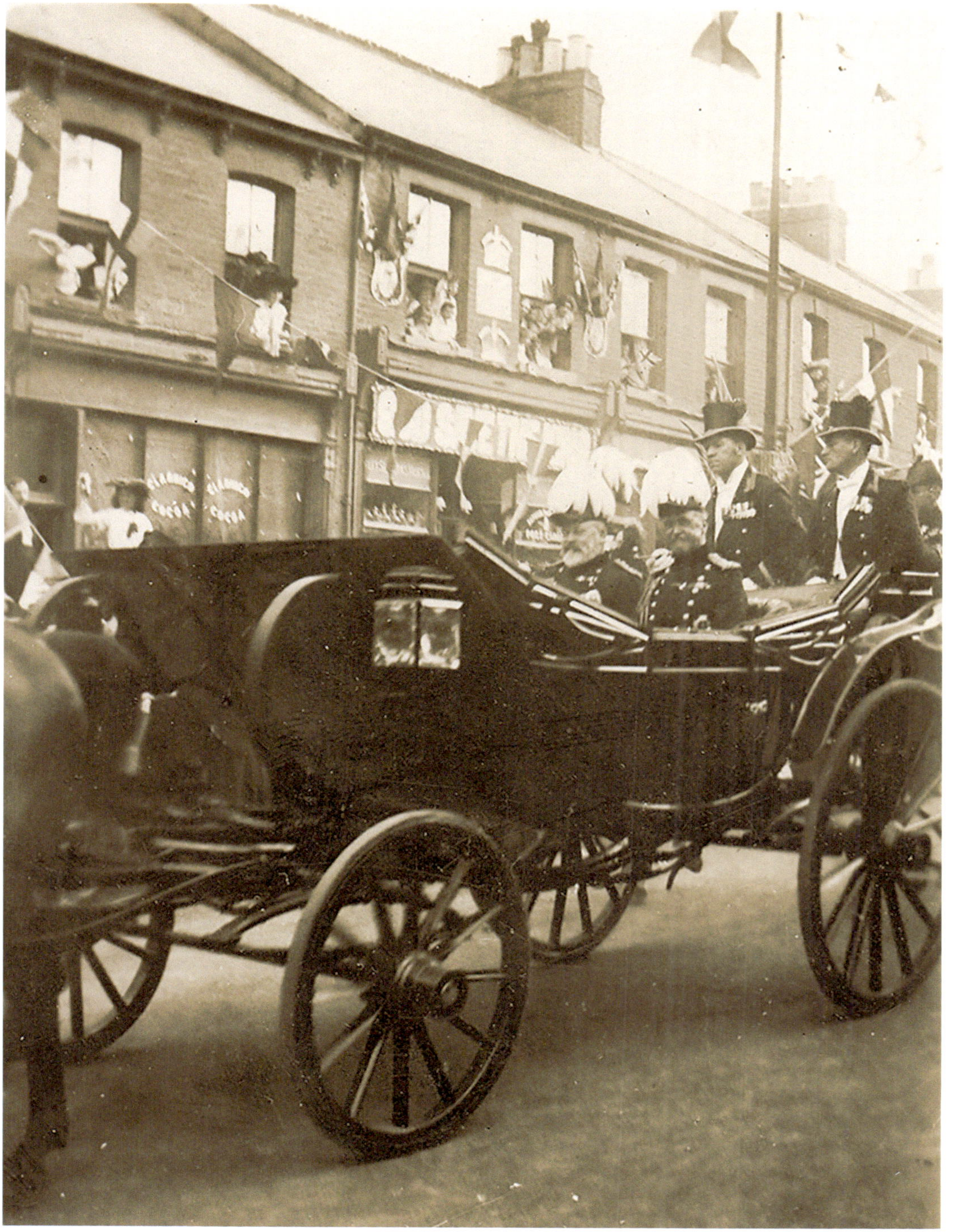

King Edward VII on his way to Gillingham on 26 July 1905 where he was to officially open the Royal Navy Hospital after first unveiling a memorial in Brompton Barracks to those killed during the Boer War (1899–1902).

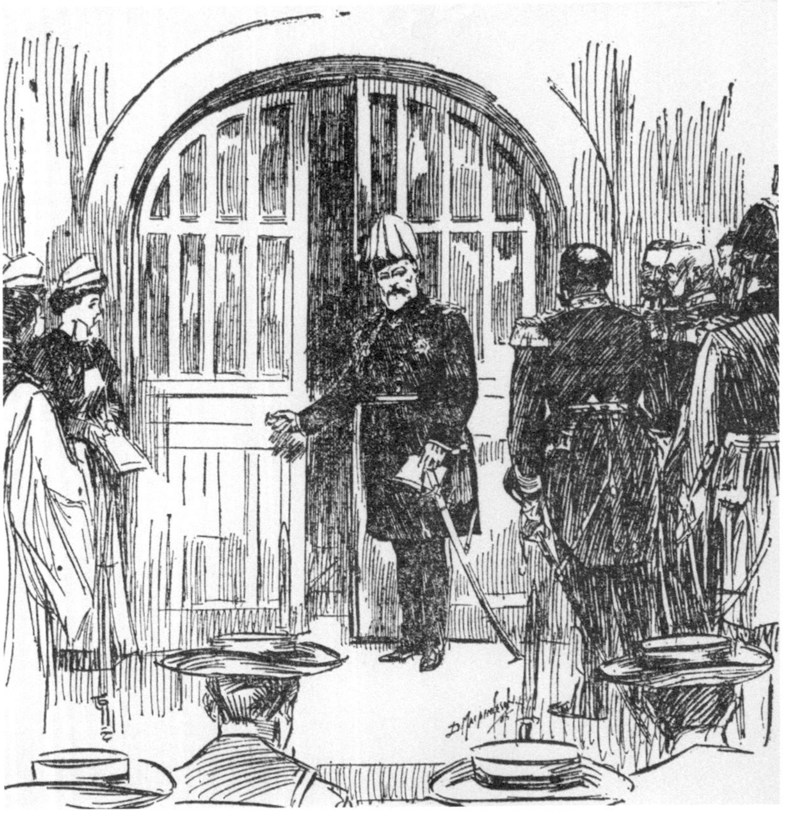

King Edward VII seen here during the official opening of the Royal Navy Hospital. Following a brief dedication and a song performed by the choir of the dockyard church, the king was given a golden key for opening the main door, loudly declaring 'this hospital now open'.

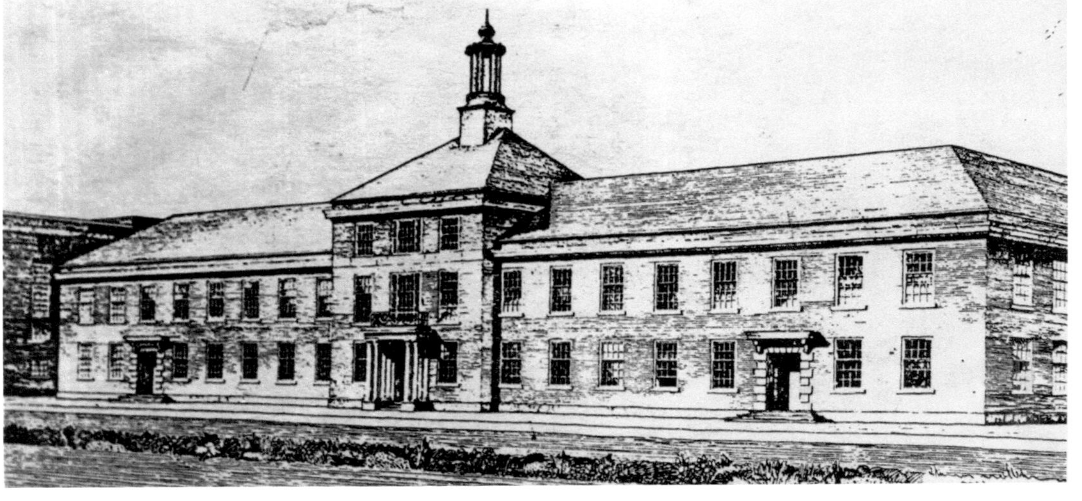

A drawing of the Municipal Building in Canterbury Street at around the time of its official opening on 25 September 1937. The building then served both the borough of Gillingham and the Kent Education Committee (Gillingham Division) prior to the formation of the Medway Towns as a unitary authority, Medway Council, in 1998. Since that time the building, now Charing House, has been converted into a privately owned care facility.

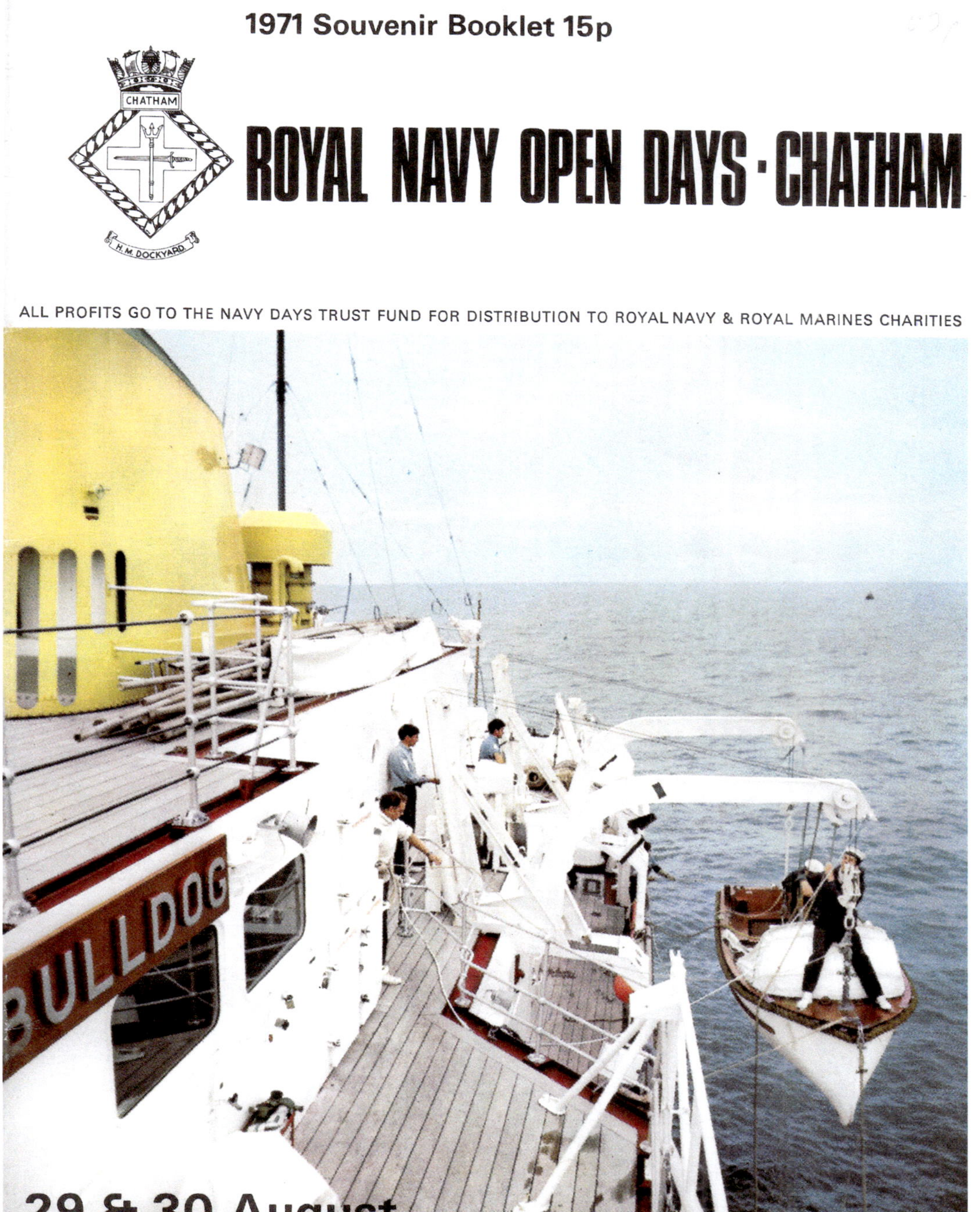

The cover for the Royal Navy Open Days held in August 1971. All the events and ships to be viewed were held in the Gillingham end of the yard, with the historic part of the yard in Chatham quite inaccessible on such occasions.

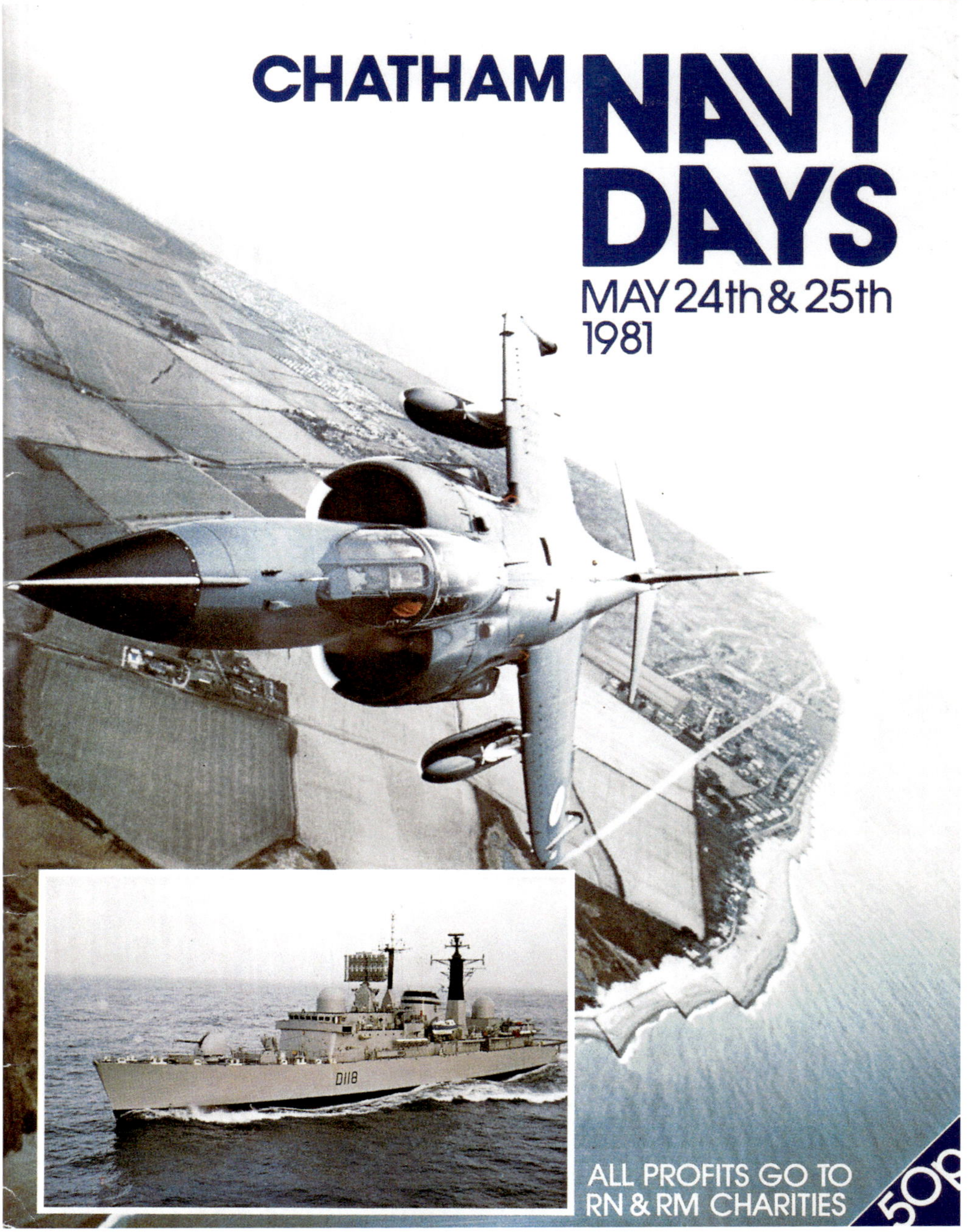

The last Navy Days, as always focussed on the Gillingham end of the yard, took place in May 1981 with a full programme of events. A further Navy Days was planned for 1982 but was unfortunately cancelled due to the Falklands conflict that had placed other requirements on those ships that might otherwise have been present on that final occasion.

About the Author

Philip MacDougall has been researching and writing about the history of Gillingham and the Medway Towns for a number of years, with his first book, *The Story of the Hoo Peninsula*, published in 1980. In all, he has written nearly twenty books on the area, including *Chatham Dockyard: The Rise and Fall of a Military Industrial Complex* (2012), *Secret Chatham* (2016), *Medway Towns at Work* (2017), *Secret Gillingham* (2019), and *Secret Rochester* (2019), together with a companion volume, *Lost Chatham*, to the present title. In the pipeline and due to be published by Amberley in 2026 is *Chatham: A Potted History*. More on Philip's books and articles written by him on the history of the Medway Towns can be found on his website: https://philipmacdougall.tilda.ws/

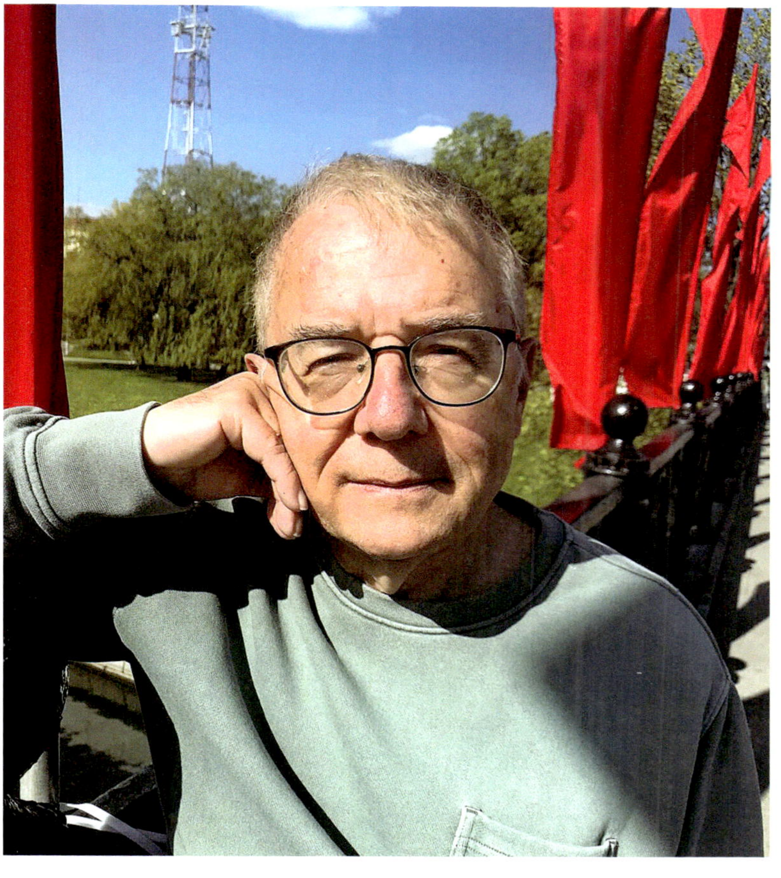